Are Evangelicals Born Again?

Are Evangelicals Born Again?

The Character Traits of True Faith

R. Kent Hughes

CROSSWAY BOOKS • WHEATON, ILLINOIS
A DIVISION OF GOOD NEWS PUBLISHERS

Are Evangelicals Born Again?

Published by Crossway Books
a division of Good News Publishers
1300 Crescent Street
Wheaton, Illinois 60187

Originally published as *Blessed Are the Born Again.*
Copyright © 1986 by Victor Books. A division of SP Publications, Inc., Wheaton, Illinois 60187

Cover design: Cindy Kiple

First printing, 1995

Printed in the United States of America

Library of Congress Cataloging-in-Publication Data
Hughes, R. Kent.
    [Blessed are the born again]
    Are evangelicals born again: the character traits of true faith /
R. Kent Hughes.
Originally published: Blessed are the born again. Wheaton, Ill.: Victor
Books, 1986.
Includes bibligraphical references.
        p.   cm.
    1. Beatitudes. I. Title.
BT382.H815 1994   241'.5—dc20   94-36901
ISBN 0-89107-798-7

03		20		01		00		99		98		97		96		95
15	14	13	12	11	10	9	8	7	6	5	4	3	2	1

To Barbara

For she is wise, if I can judge of her,
And fair she is, if that mine eyes be true,
And true she is, as she hath prov'd herself,
And therefore, like herself, wise, fair, and true,
Shall she be placed in my constant soul.
The Merchant of Venice, II.VI

TABLE OF

CONTENTS

ARE EVANGELICALS BORN AGAIN?

> *. . . those who are pure in their own eyes*
> *and yet are not cleansed of their filth.*
>
> (PROVERBS 30:12)

A re evangelicals born again? This long-smoldering question was aflame once more in my mind after the events of the day. For in a convention hotel room, I had just watched an evangelical church leader come to Christ.

The hour had left me exhausted. Initially I had been incredulous as the man recounted his enviable heritage. He was the son of a prominent theologian and minister. From childhood he had attended Christian schools and had graduated from an evangelical Christian college. He had married a Christian from another notable family. He was successful in business, a leader in his denomination, and a board member of several prestigious Christian organizations. His children were believers.

My initial incredulity faded as he carefully explained that since his youth he had sensed that he was not a believer, but conforming to conventional piety had come easy to him. As a boy he had "gone forward" and been baptized. He knew his Bible and offered admirable prayers over dinner and in public.

Yet all the while he was quietly aware, almost sardonically so, that he had never truly bent his knee to Christ—and so was not born again.

He tearfully explained that he would never have come for spiritual help if his illegal business practices had not been uncovered. He had come to the end of himself. There was nowhere to turn but to Christ—and he did. As we knelt together, I witnessed a moving, passionate outpouring of genuine contrition for sins. This man, this evangelical churchman, now believed in Christ, repented, and was truly born again.

The Question Must Be Asked

"Are evangelicals born again?" is much more than an attention-getting gimmick. It is a profoundly valid question that the evangelical establishment needs to ask.

The classical definition of *evangelical* is: one who believes the Bible is divinely inspired and infallible and who subscribes to doctrinal formulations that teach the depravity of man, the substitutionary death and atonement of Christ, salvation by unmerited grace through personal faith in Christ (not good works), the necessity of a transformed life, the existence of a literal heaven and hell, and the visible, personal return of Jesus Christ to set up His kingdom of righteousness. Moreover, he or she believes in the proclamation of the gospel and the mission of winning the world for Christ.[1] Recently, however, the term evangelical has begun to lose its classical confessional dimension and has become, in the words of Professor David Wells, "descriptively anemic." Wells adds:

> To say that someone is an evangelical says little about what they are likely to believe (although it says more if they are older and

less if they are younger). And so the term is forced to compensate for its theological weakness by borrowing meaning from adjectives the very presence of which signals the fragmentation and disintegration of the movement. What is now primary is not what is evangelical, but what is adjectivally distinctive, whether Catholic, liberationist, feminist, ecumenist, young, orthodox, radical, liberal, or charismatic. It is, I think, the dark prelude to death, when parasites have finally succeeded in bringing down their host.[2]

George Gallup's much-discussed religious survey of 1978 established one thing for certain: many evangelicals are woefully ignorant of the Bible and do not maintain beliefs or live in a way that is consonant with their evangelical profession.[3] These realities alone ought to be cause for question. But perhaps the most telling fact is that in 1990 a whopping one third of Americans claimed to be "born again," and yet their influence on culture was negligible.[4]

Jesus Himself warns us in His Parable of the Wheat and the Tares (Matthew 13:24-30) that it is the enemy's practice to sow counterfeit believers among Christ's true followers, so perfectly disguised that they will not be discovered until the harvest.

It is apparent that many have fallen to what Dietrich Bonhoeffer piquantly warns of as "cheap grace":

Cheap grace is the preaching of forgiveness without requiring repentance, baptism without church discipline, Communion without confession, absolution without personal confession. Cheap grace is grace without discipleship, grace without the cross, grace without Jesus Christ, living and incarnate.[5]

Today the sad truth is, there are multitudes of evangelicals (Bible-carrying church-attenders) who are not truly born again.

Evangelical Worldliness

Through a series of far-reaching accommodations, evangelicals have blurred the line between their faith and the ways of the world.

Cultural Accommodation

Evangelicals have drunk unconsciously from a loose set of attitudes and ideas known as modernity.[6] Their confidence in the truth of biblical revelation has been subtly eroded by the culture's insistence that objective truth cannot be known, and that all anyone can do is impose personal subjective categories onto reality. As a result evangelicals have increasingly privatized their faith and have become less concerned about its reasonableness. This retreat into self has become a fact of evangelical life. As James Davison Hunter wrote in the landmark study *Evangelicalism: The Coming Generation*:

> The fascination with the self and with human subjectivity has
> become a well-established cultural feature of evangelicalism in
> the latter part of the twentieth century, not an ephemeral fash-
> ion among the younger generation.[7]

Self-focus diminishes God-focus, so that God is increasingly relegated to the periphera of life, leaving evangelicals open to further invasions of worldliness. This is enhanced by modern life's worship of technology's brilliance, which effectively numbs moderns to the numinous and their need of God.

The overall effect of modernity upon evangelicals has been to subvert their access to God and to shape them increasingly after the world. This is mirrored in the statistical evidence that there is very little difference in the television viewing habits of Christians and non-Christians, a fact that also increases self-absorption,[8] a diminishing focus on the true God, and the descent into worldliness.

Theological Accommodation

Contemporary evangelicalism's assimilation of modernity's self-focus has had a telling effect on its theology because when the emphasis switches from God to self, theology becomes anthropology; man becomes the beginning point of theology rather than God. Theology is set against practicality.

This has become widely evident as many evangelical pulpits have abandoned biblical exposition for the homiletics of consensus—preaching the bromides of the therapeutic age for "felt needs" as determined by the pollsters' analyses. Certainly all preaching must be informed by, and sensitive to, perceived needs. But the problem with preaching only to felt needs is that often our deepest needs go far deeper than perceived needs. For example, people need to know that they are sinners (whether they feel it or not), but the extraordinary attention presently given to matters of self by evangelical Christians has softened the meaning and the implications of the traditional belief in the self's inherent sinfulness.[9] Indeed, Robert Schuller has declared that sin is not rebellion against God but rather "a lack of self-esteem."[10] Most recently, Doug Murren argued that because today's person has such low self-esteem, sermons that moved people in the nineteenth century would be inappropriate for today.[11] But perhaps the most flagrant example of theological accommodation is the hacking-up of biblical texts on the procrustean bed of therapeutic preaching as exemplified by Schuller's book *The Be Happy Attitudes*, a grotesque exegesis that presents the Beatitudes as nostrums of self-fulfillment.

When theology becomes anthropology, it becomes captive to the world, which is to say worldly.

Moral Accommodation

Professor Hunter's research reveals that "Even the words *worldly* and *worldliness* have, within a generation, lost most of their traditional meaning."[12] He notes that while the prohibitions against sexual sins are still intact, "the attitude toward those prohibitions has noticeably softened."[13] Predictably, these changes have been reflected in evangelical conduct. Doug Sherman and William Hendricks in their book *Keeping Your Ethical Edge Sharp* have shown that there is little difference between the ethical practices of professed Christians and non-Christians.[14]

So we see that evangelical accommodation is comprehensive (*cultural*, *theological*, and *moral*). Bottom line, this means that becoming an evangelical Christian can bring little or no change in one's lifestyle.

The Ease of Being Evangelical

The greatness of the problem is easily seen when we realize that it is not very difficult to be given the status of "evangelical," whether a person is born again or not. The process is essentially *cultural*. That is, display similar religious traits and you will be accepted. Here are some of the most effective:

Vocabulary

Biblical history records that when the Gileadites and the Ephraimites were warring, the Gileadites developed a password to detect Ephraimites who pretended to be Gileadites when captured. The word was *Shibboleth*, which the Ephraimites (who had trouble with the *sh* sound) could only pronounce *Sibboleth*. This tactic worked perfectly on the unsuspecting enemy (Judges 12:4-7).

We evangelicals have our Shibboleths, but unfortunately they are easy to pick up. They are words and phrases like *fellowship* and *brother* and *born again*. Use these passwords with the right inflection and you will fool most of the people most of the time.

Social Conventions

Sharing the same social attitudes is a most effective tactic. Simply put, share the same likes and dislikes (especially dislikes) and you will probably pass as an evangelical.

The ease with which you can adopt the behavioral mores of evangelical Christianity has been facilitated by the gradual alignment of many evangelicals with the materialism, hedonism, and fads of our secular culture.[15]

Heritage

If your parents are respectable Christians, or even better, Christian workers, it will probably be assumed that you are a believer. And by regularly attending church and practicing the tithe, you will place yourself beyond question.

The desire of overly anxious parents to see their children born again has contributed to this "heritage equals salvation" delusion. Some well-meaning parents have manipulated their children into bogus confessions, bogus baptisms, and bogus membership. Some of these offspring are even admitted to Christian schools on the basis of "testimonies" ghost-written by their parents.

For these and similar reasons, multitudes of unregenerate evangelicals are comfortably ensconced in their churches. And no one has the gracious temerity to question the authenticity of their faith.

The Attraction of Evangelicalism

Why would anyone ever willfully take up the "narrow way" of evangelical Christianity apart from being born again?

A major reason has already been anticipated. For many it is the path of least resistance. To do otherwise would impair comfortable family and social relationships.

Besides, evangelical Christianity has "arrived," though its arrival may be no more than an Indian summer.[16] Despite scandals, its preachers still dominate the religious media. Its recording artists sell big. A billion dollars is spent annually on its publications. Sometimes it even makes and breaks politicians. Being "born again" can be profitable. Jesus saves, but Jesus also sells. Evangelicalism is big business.

We must remember too that the biblical lifestyle is a good way to live. Families subscribing to biblical models tend to be happier and healthier and to stay together. It is not at all surprising that the wholesome, solid way of Christianity attracts those who would practice its style without knowing its inner reality.

The human race has an infinite capacity for self-delusion. And nowhere is this more perfectly demonstrated than in the lives of thousands of evangelicals who are not really born again.

What wise Solomon said of some people in his day goes for some in ours as well: ". . . those who are pure in their own eyes and yet are not cleansed of their filth" (Proverbs 30:12). Jesus tells us that a terrible surprise awaits immense numbers of such "believers" at the judgment:

> "Many will say to me on that day, 'Lord, Lord, did we not prophesy in your name, and in your name drive out demons and perform many miracles?' Then I will tell them plainly, 'I never knew you. Away from me, you evildoers!'" (Matthew 7:22-23)

John Newton, the eighteenth-century father of English evangelicalism, provides this sobering dictum that is refreshingly humble and healthy:

> If I ever reach heaven I expect to find three wonders there: first, to meet some I had not thought to see there; second, to miss

some I had thought to meet there; and third, the greatest wonder of all, to find myself there.[17]

The Beatitudes: A Gracious Remedy

On that memorable morning when the evangelical leader came to Christ, I asked him to turn to the first Beatitude and read it aloud: "Blessed are the poor in spirit, for theirs is the kingdom of heaven" (Matthew 5:3). It had an electrifying effect on him. He saw at once that he had never been poor in spirit, but rather proud and self-sufficient, and thus self-excluded from the kingdom. The truth of the first Beatitude penetrated him, broke him, and opened him to the grace of Christ.

This is what the Beatitudes do, for *they describe the inner character of those who are members of the kingdom of heaven.*

The careful reader will notice that the first and last Beatitudes begin and end with the same phrase—"for theirs is the kingdom of heaven." This is a Hebrew stylistic device called an *inclusion*, which means that everything in the Beatitudes is about the kingdom of heaven.[18] I like to call the Beatitudes "attitudes of grace," for in them we see what the heart of a true child of God is like—the truly born-again heart.

Cultural tests are, of course, of some use in determining our spiritual state, but they are certainly fallible. Theological, confessional tests are far better. However, we can confess the creeds and not be born again. We can say we believe in Christ and yet really not believe. All unregenerate evangelicals do!

But the Beatitudes are even more revealing of our spiritual state. They are functional tests of our spiritual life. If we are true believers, then *something* of each of the eight Beatitudes will be present in our lives. This is not to suggest that anyone can perfectly model the Beatitudes or be saved by living them, but rather that if one does not have something of each of the Beatitudes in his or her life—if there is no desire for the Beatitudes to become a growing personal reality—that person may well not be born again.

Do we have the life of Christ in us and therefore the character of the kingdom? The Beatitudes will tell us.

There is nothing quite like the Beatitudes in all of Scripture. They are the opening lines of the greatest sermon ever preached. Their very position makes them seminal to life. They are indicators of genuine faith. They are absolutely crucial. The Lord gives them to us in Matthew as eight consecutive spiritual H-bombs, concentrated theological epigrams that detonate with increasing effect. Each Beatitude stands upon the preceding statements, mounting a ruthless theological logic that assaults the soul with hammerlike power. The result is a graced harrowing of our souls. They expose the true state of our hearts and call us to even higher planes of holy living in demonstrating the postures of regeneration.

On Taking the Prescription

The Beatitudes provide perfect medicine for evangelicals. But we are not to use them to judge the spiritual state of others. However, though we dare not apply them to others, we also dare not refrain from applying them to ourselves.

As you undergo the tests of the Beatitudes in each of the eight succeeding chapters, my prayer is that the Holy Spirit will cause you to see yourself in God's true, gracious light.

Those of you who have been born again are in for a wild, joyous ride. The Beatitudes will take you down when you expose your soul to them. But as you yield to their sweet violence, they will take you vaulting to the heavenlies.

And to those who are not yet born again, or are unsure of where you stand, the following is tailored to settle the matter once for all. The Beatitudes will cut through the cant and jargon of religious formula. They will take you to the end of yourself. They will make you desperately thirsty for God and His righteousness, and then they will lead you to cast yourself upon Him who is your only hope.

As you begin pray, asking Him to:

- Show you Himself in all His holiness.
- Show you yourself as you really are.
- Show you His grace through the gifts of faith and repentance.

THE RICHES OF POVERTY

"Blessed are the poor in spirit,
for theirs is the kingdom of heaven."

(MATTHEW 5:3)

Those of us who grew up in the fifties are quite familiar with the name Mickey Cohen because he was the most flamboyant criminal of the day. Perhaps some have even heard of Cohen's becoming a "Christian."

The story goes like this: at the height of his career, Cohen was persuaded to attend an evangelistic service at which he showed a surprising interest in Christianity. Hearing of this, and realizing what a great influence a converted Mickey Cohen could have for the Lord, some prominent Christian leaders began visiting him in an effort to convince him to accept Christ. Late one night, after repeatedly being encouraged to open the door of his life on the basis of Revelation 3:20 ("I stand at the door and knock. If anyone hears my voice and opens the door, I will come in"), Cohen prayed.

Hopes ran high among his believing acquaintances. But with the passing of time no one could detect any change in Cohen's life. Finally they confronted him with the reality that being a Christian meant he would have to give up his friends and his profession.

Cohen demurred. His logic? There are "Christian football players, Christian cowboys, Christian politicians; why not a Christian gangster?"[1]

The absurdity of what happened to Mickey Cohen dramatically underscores what is happening to untold numbers today. Though many ostensibly have "accepted Christ," they continue life as they always have. There is no repentance. They remain self-sufficient, even puffed up. Indeed, they are nowhere near the kingdom because they have not experienced the poverty of spirit that the first Beatitude insists is the initial ground of the kingdom of heaven.

What evangelical Christianity needs is an exposure to the life-giving logic of the Beatitudes and the blessedness of their fearsome surgery.

Blessedness: The Approval of God

Each of the eight Beatitudes opens with the word "blessed." So it is essential that we understand here in the beginning what this word means, because it bears on everything that will be said in the remainder of this book.

Contrary to popular opinion, *blessed* does not mean "happy," even though some translations have rendered it this way. Happiness is a subjective state, a feeling. But Jesus is not declaring how people feel; rather, he is making an objective statement about what God thinks of them.[2] *Blessed* is a positive judgment by God on the individual that means "to be approved" or "to find approval." *So when God blesses us, He approves us.*[3]

Of course, there is no doubt that such blessing will bring feelings of happiness and that blessed people are generally happy. But we must remember that the root idea of "blessed" is an awareness of approval by God. Blessedness is not simply a nice wish from God; it is a pronouncement of what we actually are—*approved.*

Blessedness indicates the smile of God or, as Max Lucado has so beautifully put it, *The Applause of Heaven.*

As we begin this study of the Beatitudes, let us realize that if God's blessing/approval means more to us than anything else— even the approval of our friends, business acquaintances, and col- leagues—then the Beatitudes are going to penetrate our hearts, speaking to us in the deepest of ways.

The question is, do we really want His approval more than anything else? Not, do we want to be happy (as proper as that desire is)—but, do we truly want God's approval above all else?

If so, then we must heed every word of the first Beatitude, for it gives us the condition of blessing in just three words: "poor in spirit." "Blessed/approved are the poor in spirit."

It is so essential that we get off to a good start with the first Beatitude if we are to understand them all that I would like to encourage the following prayer.

Dear Lord,
I long for Your smile upon my life. So please open my heart to the
meaning of the Beatitudes.
I open myself to their light. Shine their rays into the deepest part of my
life. Sear my soul. Heal me.
Build the character of the kingdom in me, so that You can call me blessed.
Amen.

Understanding Poverty of Spirit

Let us understand what poverty of spirit is not. It is not the convic- tion that one is of no value whatsoever. It does not mean the absence of self-worth or, as one theologian put it, "ontological insignifi- cance." It does not require that we believe ourselves to be zeros. Such an attitude is simply not scriptural, for Christ's death on our behalf teaches us that we are of great value (1 Corinthians 6:20; 7:23).

Neither does "poor in spirit" mean shyness. Many people

who are naturally shy and introverted are extremely proud. Nor does "poor in spirit" mean lacking in vitality, spiritually anemic, or gutless.

Certainly, "poor in spirit" also does not refer to showy humility like that of Uriah Heep in Charles Dickens's *David Copperfield*, who kept reminding people that he was a "very humble person."

The great British preacher Martyn Lloyd-Jones tells of meeting such a man on one of his preaching missions. When Dr. Lloyd-Jones arrived at the train station, the man asked for the minister's suitcase and in fact almost ripped it from his hand saying, "I am a deacon in the church where you are preaching tomorrow. . . . You know, I am a mere nobody, a very unimportant man. Really. I do not count; I am not a great man in the church; I am just one of those men who carry the bag for the minister."

Lloyd-Jones observes, "He was anxious that I should know what a humble man he was, how 'poor in spirit.' Yet by his anxiety to make it known, he was denying the very thing he was trying to establish. Uriah Heep—the man who thus, as it were, glories in his poverty of spirit and thereby proves he is not humble."[4] We all have met this kind of person, who by his own self-conscious diffidence is begging for us to say that he is not really nothing but actually quite wonderful. When this attitude is present, there is an absence of poverty of spirit.

What, then, does "poor in spirit" mean? The history of the Greek word for "poor," *ptochos*, provides some insight. It comes from a verbal root that denotes "to cower and cringe like a beggar." In classical Greek *ptochos* came to mean "someone who crouches about, wretchedly begging." In the New Testament it bears something of this idea because it denotes a poverty so deep that the person must obtain his living by begging. He is fully dependent on the giving of others. He cannot survive without help from the outside. Thus an excellent translation is "beggarly poor."

Now, if we take this meaning and combine it with the following words ("in spirit") we have the idea, "Blessed are the *beggarly poor in spirit*." The sense is: "Blessed are those who are so desperately poor in their spiritual resources that they realize they must have help from outside sources."

"Poverty of Spirit, then, is the personal acknowledgment of spiritual bankruptcy."[5] It is the awareness and admission that we are utterly sinful and without the moral virtues adequate to commend us to God. John Wesley said of the poor in spirit, "He has a deep sense of the loathsome leprosy of sin which he brought with him from his mother's womb, which overspreads his whole soul, and totally corrupts every power and faculty thereof."[6]

It is the recognition of our personal moral unworthiness. The "poor in spirit" see themselves as spiritually needy. My favorite rendering of the verse is:

> Blessed are those who realize that they have nothing within themselves to commend them to God, for theirs is the kingdom of heaven.

The World Rejects Poverty of Spirit

Poverty of spirit is the antithesis of the proud selfishness and self-sufficiency of today's world. The world has its own ideas of blessedness. "Blessed is the man who is always right." "Blessed is the man who is strong." "Blessed is the man who rules." "Blessed is the man who is satisfied with himself." "Blessed is the man who is rich." "Blessed is the man who is popular."

Today's men and women think that the answer to life is found in self. Actress Shirley MacLaine is not alone in her journey into self. Many in the church travel with her. Karl Jung is their Virgil, and the subterranean god of self is their Inferno. Christian narcissism is promoted as biblical self-love. King Jesus becomes the imperial self. When this happens, Christianity suffers a massive shrinkage, as David Wells explains:

> Theology becomes therapy. . . . The biblical interest in right-
> eousness is replaced by a search for happiness, holiness by
> wholeness, truth by feeling, ethics by feeling good about one's
> self. . . . The past recedes. The Church recedes. The world
> recedes. All that remains is self.[7]

Someday, if history is allowed to continue, a perceptive artist may sculpt a statue of twentieth-century man with his arms draped about his inflated self in loving embrace, kissing his mirror image.

To this, Jesus answers, "Blessed (approved of God) are the poor in spirit, for theirs is the kingdom of heaven."

Poverty of Spirit Is Essential for Knowing God's Approval

We must understand and embrace a true poverty of spirit, for that is the only way we can ever know God's smile. David became the greatest king of Israel, and the key to his rise to greatness was his poverty of spirit. Listen to his words when it all began: "Who am I, and what is my family or my father's clan in Israel, that I should become the king's son-in-law?" (1 Samuel 18:18). Later in life, before his fall, he said, "Who am I, O Sovereign LORD, and what is my family, that you have brought me this far?" (2 Samuel 7:18).

Similarly, Gideon, whom we celebrate for his amazing deliv-erance of Israel with just 300 men, began with these words: "But Lord . . . how can I save Israel? My clan is the weakest in Manasseh, and I am the least in my family" (Judges 6:15).

Significantly, when Jesus began His public ministry He opened the scroll to Isaiah 61:1 and began with this opening line: "The Spirit of the Lord is on me, because he has anointed me to preach good news to the poor" (see Luke 4:18). In Isaiah's context the poor were the exiled people of Israel who had not compromised and who looked alone to God to save them and establish His king-dom. These are always the people to whom He comes. The incar-nate Son of God was born of a woman who sang, "My soul glorifies the Lord and my spirit rejoices in God my Savior, for he has been mindful of the humble state of his servant" (Luke 1:46-47). When Christ was born, the angels announced it to humble shepherds, not to the Establishment (Luke 2:8-15). And when Jesus was presented in the Temple, aged Simeon and Anna, representatives of the poor of Isaiah's prophecy, exalted God because of Him (Luke 2:25-38). These are the people to whom Christ is born, and *in* whom He is born. Lay this to heart: "The LORD is close to the brokenhearted and saves those who are crushed in spirit" (Psalm 34:18). This is the way it will always be.

Poverty of Spirit Is Essential for Salvation

Poverty of spirit is an indispensable sign of grace. No one can truly know Christ without it. There are most likely scores of evangelicals in your own community, prominent "Christians," who do not know Christ. They are tares amidst wheat who perhaps do not even know it (Matthew 13:24-30). They have never come to a blessed emptiness, to the very end of themselves. They have never confessed, "There is nothing in me to commend me to God"; and thus they are lost.

The changeless truth is, no one can come to Christ without poverty of spirit. This is not to say that one must have a *perfect* sense of one's spiritual insufficiency to be saved. Very few, if any, come to this. Rather, it means that the spiritually proud and self-sufficient, those who actually think there is something within them that will make God accept them—these people are lost.

Positively stated, "Those who acknowledge themselves as spiritually bankrupt enter the kingdom of heaven." No one enters God's kingdom without such an acknowledgment, regardless of how many times he or she has walked the aisle, raised a hand, signed a decision card, prayed "the sinner's prayer," or given his or her testimony.

Salvation is by faith alone, *sola fide* (Ephesians 2:8-9; Romans 11:6);[8] but poverty of spirit is the posture of faith. God pours out His grace to the spiritually bankrupt, for only they are open to believe and receive His grace and salvation. He does this with no one else. No one can enter the kingdom without poverty of spirit.

Poverty of Spirit Is Essential for Spiritual Growth

We never outgrow the first Beatitude, even though it is the basis by which we ascend to the others. In fact, if we outgrow it, we have outgrown our Christianity—we are post-Christian.

That is what was happening in the Laodicean church. Christ rebuked that failing church with these stern words:

> "You say, 'I am rich; I have acquired wealth and do not need a thing.' But you do not realize that you are wretched, pitiful, poor, blind and naked. I counsel you to buy from me gold refined in the fire, so you can become rich; and white clothes to wear, so you can cover your shameful nakedness; and salve to put on your eyes, so you can see." (Revelation 3:17-18)

Just as no one can come to Christ without poverty of spirit, no one can continue to grow apart from an ongoing poverty of spirit.

Poverty of spirit is foundational because a continual sense of spiritual need is the basis for ongoing spiritual blessing. A perpetual awareness of our spiritual insufficiency opens us to continually receiving spiritual riches. Poverty of spirit is something we never outgrow. In fact, the more spiritually mature we become, the more profound will be our sense of poverty.

It is because of this that every believer should commit the Beatitudes to memory and make the first Beatitude, especially, his or her conscious refrain: "Blessed are the beggarly poor in spirit"; "blessed are the spiritually bankrupt, for theirs is the kingdom of heaven."

The Riches of Poverty

Now we turn to the statement of the reward: "for theirs is the kingdom of heaven." "Theirs" is emphatic. It means theirs in the sense of *theirs alone*, barring all others who approach God with a different spirit than that of beggarliness.[9] Again, none but those who are "poor in spirit" will enter the kingdom of heaven.

The reward of the kingdom is both now and future. It is present because all who have life are in the kingdom now. We are seated with Christ in the heavenly places *now* (Ephesians 2:6). We are subjects of Christ *now*. We are overcomers *now*. We are a kingdom of priests *now*. This means we are kings and queens, and that we reign in life and exercise vast authority and power. It means that our poverty of spirit, our weakness, is a reservoir of authority and power. Our weakness is the occasion for His power, our inadequacy for His adequacy, our poverty for His riches, our inarticulation for His articulation, our tentativeness for His confidence (see 2 Corinthians 12:9-10; Colossians 2:9-10).

As kings and queens, we are also free. Pride makes slaves out of all whom it possesses; not so with poverty of spirit. We are free to be full of God, free to be all that He would have us to be, free to be ourselves. We reign now and for all eternity. The kingdom is ours—ours alone!

Crucial Teaching

The supreme lesson of this Beatitude is that without poverty of spirit no one enters the kingdom of heaven. Its prominent position—as the opening sentence of the Sermon on the Mount—declares for all time that no one is saved who believes there is something within him that will make God prefer or accept him.

Self-righteousness, moral pride, vain presumption will damn the soul! Jesus made this crystal-clear with the account of the tax-gatherer and the Pharisee who went up to the Temple to pray:

"Two men went up to the temple to pray, one a Pharisee and the other a tax collector. The Pharisee stood up and prayed about himself: 'God, I thank you that I am not like other men—robbers, evildoers, adulterers—or even like this tax collector. I fast twice a week and give a tenth of all I get.' But the tax collector stood at a distance. He would not even look up to heaven, but beat his breast and said, 'God, have mercy on me, a sinner.' I tell you that this man, rather than the other, went home justified before God. For everyone who exalts himself will be humbled, and he who humbles himself will be exalted." (Luke 18:10-14)

We must realize that:

The first link between
  my soul and Christ is
not my goodness
  but my badness;
not my merit
  but my misery;
not my standing
  but my falling.

Fortunately, this truth can penetrate the most privileged of hearts, as it did to one of England's distinguished jurists. The church he attended had three mission churches under its care. On the first Sunday of the new year all the members of the missions came to the big city church for a combined Communion service. In those mission churches, which were located in the slums of the city, were some outstanding cases of conversions—thieves, burglars, and so on—but all knelt side by side at the Communion rail.

On one such occasion the pastor saw a former thief kneeling beside the aforementioned jurist, a judge of the High Court of England. After his release the thief had been converted and became a Christian worker. Yet, as the judge and the former thief knelt together, neither seemed to be aware of the other.

After the service, the judge happened to walk out with the pastor and said, "Did you notice who was kneeling beside me at the Communion rail this morning?"

The pastor replied, "Yes, but I didn't think that you did."

The two walked along in silence for a few more moments, when the judge declared, "What a miracle of grace."

The pastor nodded in agreement. "Yes, what a marvelous miracle of grace."

Then the judge asked, "But to whom do you refer?"

The pastor responded, "Why, to the conversion of that convict."

"But I was not referring to him. I was thinking of myself," explained the judge.

Surprised, the pastor replied, "You were thinking of yourself? I don't understand."

"Yes," the judge went on. "It was natural for the burglar to respond to God's grace when he came out of jail. His life was nothing but a desperate history of crime, and when he saw the Savior he knew there was salvation and hope and joy for him. He understood how much he needed that help.

"But I . . . I was taught from earliest infancy to be a gentleman—that my word was my bond, that I was to say my prayers, go to church, receive Communion. I went up to Oxford, took my degrees, was called to the bar, and eventually ascended to judge. My friend, it was God's grace that drew me; it was God's grace that opened my heart to receive Christ. I'm a greater miracle of His grace."

Listen again to Jesus' words, "Blessed (approved of God) are the (beggarly) poor in spirit, for theirs is the kingdom of heaven (now and forevermore)."

The question I must ask is, have you experienced true poverty of spirit? Can you say,

Nothing in my hand I bring,
  Simply to Thy cross I cling;
Naked, come to Thee for dress
  Helpless, look to Thee for grace;
Foul, I to the fountain fly;
  Wash me, Saviour, or I die.

(AUGUSTUS M. TOPLADY,1740-1778)

Is this your heart's cry? Or are you a church attender without Christ? Are you an unregenerate evangelical? Are you a Christless "Christian"? If so, hear God's Word and take it to heart: "Blessed are the poor in spirit, for theirs is the kingdom of heaven."

The other great lesson for all who are born again, regardless of their spiritual maturity, is that poverty of spirit is necessary for continuing spiritual blessing.

I personally can say that the most profitable spiritual experiences of my life have come out of times of profound spiritual poverty, times when God has brought me face to face with the fact of my need, times when I once again realized there was nothing within me to commend me to Him. Sometimes He has done this through professional failure, sometimes through intellectual shortcomings, sometimes through social or family pressures.

Whatever the case, in Him my bankruptcy has been the opening for His riches. And it can be yours as well. "Blessed are the poor in spirit, for theirs is the kingdom of heaven."

Lord, we long for Your smile even as we acknowledge our own spiritual bankruptcy!

CHAPTER THREE

THE COMFORT OF
MOURNING

"Blessed are those who mourn,
for they will be comforted."

(MATTHEW 5:4)

Charles Colson, in his brilliant book of essays *Who Speaks for God?*, tells of watching a segment of television's "60 Minutes" in which host Mike Wallace interviewed Auschwitz survivor Yehiel Dinur, a principal witness at the Nuremburg war-crime trials.

During the interview, a film clip from Adolf Eichmann's 1961 trial was viewed that showed Dinur entering the courtroom and coming face to face with Eichmann for the first time since being sent to Auschwitz almost twenty years earlier. Stopped cold, Dinur began to sob uncontrollably and then fainted while the presiding judge pounded his gavel for order.

"Was Dinur overcome by hatred? Fear? Horrid memories?" asks Colson, who then answers:

> No; it was none of these. Rather, as Dinur explained to Wallace, all at once he realized Eichmann was not the godlike army offi-cer who had sent so many to their deaths. This Eichmann was

an ordinary man. "I was afraid about myself," said Dinur. "I saw that I am capable to do this. I am . . . exactly like he."

Wallace's subsequent summation of Dinur's terrible discovery—"Eichmann is in all of us"—is a horrifying statement; but it indeed captures the central truth about man's nature. For as a result of the Fall, sin is in each of us—not just the susceptibility to sin, but sin itself.[1]

Colson follows his penetrating observation with this question: why is it that today sin is so seldom written or preached about? The answer is in Dinur's dramatic collapse, for to truly confront the sin within us is a devastating experience. If sin was preached on, says Colson, many would flee their church pews never to return.[2]

The abiding fact is that man has always been in need of such an encounter. And to this end Jesus has given the second Beatitude, because it shows the necessity of truly facing one's sin.

So no one would miss the point, the Lord put this in the most striking language.

Truth Upside-down

When read apart from its context the second Beatitude is startling: "Blessed are those who mourn, for they will be comforted." This is, of course, a paradox—and it is meant to grab us.

G. K. Chesterton once defined a paradox as "truth standing on its head calling for attention," and this is certainly true here. Jesus states one of the essential truths of life in such a way that it cries for all to come and take a good long look, a look that can bring life. "Blessed/approved are those who mourn."

The intimate connection of this second Beatitude with the first is beautiful and compelling. The first Beatitude, "Blessed are the poor in spirit," is primarily *intellectual* (those who understand that they are spiritual beggars are blessed); the second Beatitude, "Blessed are those who mourn," is its *emotional* counterpart. It naturally follows that when we see ourselves for what we are, our emotions will be stirred to mourning.

Again, as with the previous Beatitude, we cannot place enough stress on the importance of these spiritual truths as they relate to the gospel. The Beatitudes are *not* the gospel because they do not explicitly explain Christ's atoning death and resurrection and how one may receive Him. But they are *preparatory* to the gospel.

The Beatitudes are preparatory in the sense that they slay us so that we may live. They hold us up against God's standards for the kingdom so that we can see our need and fly to Him. They cut through the delusions of formula Christianity and expose the shallowness of evangelicals who can give all the "right" answers but do not know Christ.

The Blessed Paradox

To begin with, what does the paradoxical pronouncement "Blessed are those who mourn" mean? Let us first note what it does not mean.

Jesus does not mean, "Blessed are grim, cheerless Christians." Some believers have apparently interpreted it this way. The Victorian preacher Charles Spurgeon once remarked that some preachers he had known appeared to have their neckties twisted around their souls.[3] Robert Louis Stevenson must have known some preachers like that because he once wrote, ironically, in his diary, "I've been to church today and am not depressed." Christ certainly is not pronouncing a Beatitude on a forlorn disposition.

Neither does Jesus mean, "Blessed are those who are mourning over the difficulties of life." The Bible does not say that mourning by itself is a blessed state. Sorrow is not blessed any more than laughter is. In fact, some mourning is cursed. For example, Amnon mourned because his lust was not fulfilled by Tamar (2 Samuel 13:2). Also, Ahab mourned because he wanted but couldn't get Naboth's vineyard (1 Kings 21:4).

Mourning over Sin

A great day has come when we see our sinful state for what it is apart from God's grace and begin to mourn over its devastating dimensions in our souls, words, and deeds as described in Romans chapter 3.

- *Souls*: "There is no one righteous, not even one; there is no one who understands, no one who seeks God. All have turned away, they have together become worthless; there is no one who does good, not even one" (vv. 10-12).
- *Words*: "Their throats are open graves; their tongues practice deceit"; "the poison of vipers is on their lips"; "their mouths are full of cursing and bitterness" (vv. 13-14).
- *Deeds*: "Their feet are swift to shed blood; ruin and misery mark their ways, and the way of peace they do not know" (vv. 15-17).

Such are we all if left to ourselves. There is always room for deprovement if we refuse the grace of God.

But it is an even greater day when we are truly confronted with our individual sins, when we refuse to rationalize them, when we reject facile euphemisms, when we call sin "sin" in our lives. And it is the greatest of all days yet when in horror and desolation over our sin and sins we weep, so that the divine smile begins to break.

Mourning over the Sins of the World

Such personal mourning is naturally expansive because one who truly mourns over his own sins will also sorrow over the power and effects of sin in the world. David mourned for the sins of others in Psalm 119:136: "Streams of tears flow from my eyes, for your law is not obeyed." The great characteristic of Jeremiah, the Weeping Prophet, was that he wept for his people (Jeremiah 9:1; 13:17).

Of course, our sinless Lord Jesus was also deeply grieved by sin in the world. Through the mystery of the Incarnation His heart became a spiritual seismograph, registering the slightest tremors of the earth's pain and sorrow. No wonder some thought Jesus was Jeremiah returned from the grave (Matthew 16:14).

Now we begin to see the force of the brilliant paradox of the second Beatitude. The Lord Jesus has stood truth on its head, and it shouts for us to take notice and understand. "Blessed/approved are those who mourn (over sin—that is their own sin and the sin that poisons the world), for they will be comforted." Christ shouts for our understanding. Blessed are we if we hear and put our understanding to work.

Mourning Is Not Popular

It is very important to see that mourning is definitely not in vogue today, despite its necessity for spiritual health. However, before elaborating on this point we must emphasize that humor and laughter are good and necessary for the believer. Solomon says that a merry heart acts as a "good medicine" (Proverbs 17:22), and we have found this to be true. Abraham Lincoln said, "If I did not laugh, I would die." The need for laughter in the church was underlined by missionary statesman Oswald Sanders with these questions:

> Should we not see that lines of laughter about the eyes are just as much marks of faith as are the lines of care and seriousness? Is laughter pagan? We have already allowed too much that is good to be lost to the church and cast many pearls before swine. A church is in a bad way when it banishes laughter from the sanctuary and leaves it to the cabaret, the nightclub, and the toastmasters.[4]

Laughter is essential, but the world despises sorrow so much that it has gone wild in its attempt to avoid it. Moderns have structured their lives to maximize entertainment and amusement in an attempt to make life one big party. They laugh when there is no reason to laugh. In fact, they laugh when they ought to cry.

Solomon was right that a merry heart acts like a "good medicine." But that does not mean you cannot overdose! Much of our culture has overdosed on amusement, as Neil Postman has so convincingly chronicled in his highly regarded *Amusing Ourselves to Death*.

The world thinks mourners (those who mourn the course of the world, who mourn sin) are mad. John Wesley observed that they consider it ". . . to be more moping and melancholy, if not downright lunacy and distraction."[5] Some have actually argued that Martin Luther was insane because of his deep mourning over his sin before his new birth. They judge his behavior as psychotic. Indeed, the world regards pain of heart with suspicion and restraint.

The church is much the same. Some actually hold that if we are good Christians, filled with the Spirit, we will experience no sorrow and will wear eternal beatific smiles like plastic Mona Lisas.

I personally know of preachers who though they maintain that they belong in the evangelical tradition never mention sin in their preaching because that makes people unhappy. The result is a Christianity that is pathetically shallow—if indeed it is Christianity at all!

True Christianity manifests itself in what we cry over and what we laugh about. So often we laugh at the things that we should weep over and weep over the things we should laugh about. In our heart of hearts, what do we weep about? What do we laugh about?

Good Mourning!

In matters of spiritual life and health, mourning is not optional. Spiritual mourning is necessary for salvation. No one is truly a

Christian who has not mourned over his or her sins. You cannot be forgiven if you are not sorry for your sins.

This was powerfully argued in the article "There Is One Thing Worse than Sin," which first appeared in the *Chicago Sun-Times*. In it, Dr. Thomas F. Roeser compared the equally reprehensible sins of Congressmen Daniel Crane and Gerald Studds. Both had been censured by the House of Representatives—Crane for having sexual relations with a seventeen-year-old female page and Studds for having relations with a seventeen-year-old male page. Roeser observed:

> Being censured is the only thing Crane and Studds have in common. The nation got a glimmer of their philosophical differences when Crane admitted tearfully to his district, then to the full House, that he "broke the laws of God and man," casting a vote for his own censure, facing the House as the Speaker announced the tally. Studds, in contrast, acknowledged he was gay in a dramatic speech to the House, then defended the relationship with the page as "mutual and voluntary." He noted that he had abided by the age of consent, and said the relationship didn't warrant the "attention or action" of the House. Studds voted "present" on the censure and heard the verdict from the Speaker with his back to the House.

Roeser went on to contrast the different moral traditions both these men represent—properly excusing neither one for his sin.

> But there's one consolation for Crane. His . . . philosophy teaches that there is one thing worse than sin. That is denial of sin, which makes forgiveness impossible.[6]

The saddest thing in life is not a sorrowing heart, but a heart that is incapable of grief over sin, for it is without grace. Without poverty of spirit no one enters the kingdom of God. Likewise, without its emotional counterpart—grief over sin—no one receives the comfort of forgiveness and salvation.

Good Grief!

If you have never sorrowed over sin in your life (not just its consequences, but sin itself), then consider long and carefully whether you really are a Christian. Genuine believers, those who are truly born again, have mourned, and continue to mourn, over sin.

For Christians, mourning over sin is essential to spiritual health. The verb used here is the most intensive of the nine verbs employed in the New Testament for mourning, and it is continuous.[7] Godly believers, therefore, perpetually mourn, and thus perpetually repent of their sins.

It is significant that the first of Martin Luther's famous *95 Theses* states that the entire life is to be one of continuous repentance and contrition. It was this attitude in the Apostle Paul that caused him to affirm, well along into his Christian life, that he was the chief of sinners (1 Timothy 1:15).

What is the result of our mourning? In the first Beatitude we saw that an ongoing poverty of spirit leaves us open to ongoing blessings of the kingdom. Here, our ongoing mourning opens us to His unspeakable comfort and joy.

This naturally anticipates and introduces the paradoxical reward: ". . . for they will be comforted."

The Comfort of Mourning

Notice that the comfort is actually immediate. Don't misinterpret the future tense, which is used merely to sequence mourning and comfort. The actual sense of Christ's words is, "Blessed are the mourners, for they shall be immediately comforted, and they will continue to be so."

Forgiveness

Notice, above all, that the basis of comfort is forgiveness. Believers are the only people in the world who are free from the guilt of their sins. The word "they" is emphatic. The sense is: "Blessed are those who mourn, for *they alone* will be comforted." We actually know we are mourners if we have the paradoxically comforting sense of God's forgiveness.

This forgiveness is also accompanied by changed lives, diminishing the sources of so much personal sorrow—arrogance, judgmentalism, selfishness, jealousy, to name a few. Therefore, comfort springs from within—from changed lives.

The Holy Spirit

The very Greek word used here for "they will be comforted" has the root from which we get *paraclete*, which is also used for the Holy Spirit, the One who comes alongside and comforts us. God's comfort is relational. It comes in the form of His divine companionship. He is our ally. He personally binds up our sorrows and consoles us.

How comprehensive our comfort is! It is immediate. It comes to us alone. It comes personally in the Person of the Holy Spirit. And it is based on the forgiveness of our sins. That is why we are called "blessed."

What a stupendous paradox. Jesus stands truth on its head to get our attention, and He says, "Would you be comforted? Then mourn. Would you be happy? Then weep."

Salvation

To those who are not yet believers, perhaps unsaved evangelicals, understand that this paradox is meant to lead you to salvation. If a spirit of mourning is welling up within you, then let your mourning elevate you to Him.

Do as the prodigal son did. He recognized his condition and mourned over it and in the midst of his misery said:

> "I will set out and go back to my father and say to him: Father, I have sinned against heaven and against you. I am no longer worthy to be called your son; make me like one of your hired men." So he got up and went to his father. But while he was still a long way off, his father saw him and was filled with compassion for him; he ran to his son, threw his arms around him and kissed him. (Luke 15:18-20)

Do you acknowledge that there is nothing within you to commend you to God? Are you mourning? Do you ache with the guilt of your sin before God and man? If so, and if you are a Christian, return to the Lord and be restored to fellowship. If you are not a believer, come to Him now and He will give you the kingdom. He will put His robe on your shoulders, His ring on your hand, His sandals on your feet, and will prepare a feast for you. You will be comforted!

That is what He has done for Charles Colson and multitudes of others. Colson says of his own experience:

> That night when I . . . sat alone at my car, my own sin—not just dirty politics, but the hatred and evil so deep within me—was thrust before my eyes, forcefully and painfully. For the first time in my life, I felt unclean, and worst of all, I could not escape. In those moments of clarity I found myself driven irresistibly into the arms of the living God.[8]

Charles Colson followed his mourning to God. And so can you. Be comforted now!

THE STRENGTH OF GENTLENESS

"Blessed are the meek,
for they will inherit the earth."

(MATTHEW 5:5)

Two men faced each other on the pavement before the governor's palace. One was Jesus Christ, the meekest man who ever lived. The other was Pontius Pilate, a man of extraordinary pride.

Jesus appeared as the epitome of weakness, a poor Jew caught on the inexorable tides of Roman history, frail and impotent, a man destined to be obliterated from the earth. Pilate was the personification of Roman power. The tides of history were with him. As part of Rome, he was heir to the earth.

The two figures are the antipodes of a tragic paradox. Jesus Christ, the prisoner, was the free man. He was in absolute control. Jesus, the meek, would inherit not only the earth but the universe. On the other hand, Pilate, the governor, was the prisoner of his own pride. He could not even control his soul. He had no inheritance.

Jesus not only taught the paradox "Blessed are the meek, for they will inherit the earth"—He lived it.

Christ was master of the paradox. His teaching is salted with shining contrasts like:

> *Last is first.*
> *Giving is receiving.*
> *Dying is living.*
> *Losing is finding.*
> *Least is greatest.*
> *Poor is rich.*
> *Weakness is strength.*
> *Serving is ruling.*

For Christ, paradoxes were an especially effective way of getting people to see essential spiritual truth—in this instance, "Blessed are the meek, for they will inherit the earth."

The beauty of a paradox is that it grabs our attention because it falls on the ear with an elevating dissonance. In the case of Matthew 5:5, it seems far truer to say, "Blessed are the proud, the intimidating, for they shall inherit the earth." But Jesus is teaching the survival not of the fittest but of the meekest! How in the world are the meek going to inherit anything? Life simply doesn't work that way. Jesus' Beatitude contravenes the laws of nature—and of society. Just look at those who occupy the executive suites—the strong, the self-sufficient, the overbearing, the capable, the aggressive, the ambitious. The world belongs to the "John Waynes." It belongs to those who proudly intone:

> *Out of the night that covers me,*
> *Black as the Pit from pole to pole,*
> *I thank whatever gods may be*
> *For my unconquerable soul.*[1]

The last thing the average man wants to be known for is meekness.

It seems that Jesus has made a great mistake, but of course we know that our Lord did not. Indeed this Beatitude provides an infallible law of life and a remarkable power for living and dying.

Tender Steel

So to begin, what does "Blessed are the meek" mean? Specifically, what does the word "meek"—or as many translations have it, "gentle"—mean?

Understand first that meekness is *not* weakness. It doesn't denote cowardice or spinelessness or timidity or the willingness to have peace at any cost. Neither does meekness suggest indecisiveness, wishy-washiness, or a lack of confidence. Meekness does not imply shyness or a withdrawn personality, as contrasted with that of an extrovert. Nor can meekness be reduced to mere niceness.

Bearing this in mind, we must note that the Greek word's development in classical literature and its other usages in the New Testament absolutely confirm the popular translations of *meek* and *gentle*.

In classical Greek the word was used to describe tame animals, soothing medicine, a mild word, and a gentle breeze.[2] "It is a word with a caress in it."[3] The New Testament bears the same sense. John Wycliffe translated the third Beatitude, "Blessed be mild men."[4] *Gentleness* and *meekness* are, indeed, caressing words.

Meekness/gentleness also implies self-control. Aristotle explained that it is the mean between excessive anger and excessive angerlessness. So the man who is meek is able to balance his anger. It is is strength under control.[5] The meek person is strong! He is gentle, meek, and mild, but he is in control. He is as strong as steel.

Trusting Steel

A reading of Psalm 37 shows that Jesus consciously alluded to verse 11, "But the meek will inherit the land," when He formulated the third Beatitude. This statement's location in the heart of this great

Psalm is deeply revelatory of what meekness/gentleness rests upon. The Israelites to whom the Psalm was written, despite living in the land, did not truly possess it because of the working of evil men. What were they to do? In a word, *trust* ("trust," vv. 3, 5; "be still . . . wait," v. 7). Thus a deep trust in the sovereign power of God is the key to meekness.

Gentle Jesus Himself forever displayed the dynamic of trust that is part and parcel of meekness. "When," as Peter records, "they hurled their insults at him, he did not retaliate; when he suffered, he made no threats. Instead, he entrusted himself to him who judges justly" (1 Peter 2:23).

Jesus' Meekness

Jesus said of Himself, "I am gentle and humble in heart" (Matthew 11:29). As the incarnation of meekness, He displayed it in two ways, both of which showed His power.

In respect to His own person, He practiced neither retaliation nor vindictiveness. When He was mocked and spat upon, He answered nothing, for He trusted His Father. As we have noted, when He was confronted by Pilate, He kept silent. When His friends betrayed Him and fled, He uttered no reproach. When Peter denied Him, Jesus restored him. When Judas came and kissed Him in Gethsemane, Jesus called him "friend." And Jesus meant it. He was never insincere. Even in the throes of death, He pleaded, "Father, forgive them, for they do not know what they are doing" (Luke 23:34). In all of this Jesus, meek and mild, was in control. He radiated power.

Yet, when it came to matters of faith and the welfare of others, Jesus was a lion. He rebuked the Pharisees' hardness of heart when He healed the man's withered hand on the Sabbath (Matthew 12:9-45). He was angered when His disciples tried to prevent little children from coming to Him (Mark 10:13-16). Jesus

46

made a whip and drove the moneychangers from the temple (John 2:14-17). He called Peter "Satan" after the outspoken fisherman tried to deter Him from His heavenly mission (Matthew 16:21-23). All of this came from Jesus, the incarnation of gentleness.

Bringing this all together, we have an amazing picture. The one who is meek has a gentle spirit because he trusts God. Indeed, there is a caress about his presence. At the same time the meek person possesses immense strength and self-control, which he exhibits in extending love rather than retaliation against those who do him evil. He stands up fearlessly in defense of others or of the truth as the occasion arises.

Jesus' Smile

Our Lord's words "Blessed are the meek" make it clear that a gentle and meek spirit has the divine approval. Therefore the presence or lack of such is indicative of one's spiritual status.

Of course, no one perfectly manifests meekness in his or her life. No one's life is a perpetual caress. No one is so strong that his or her only response is love. No one totally escapes pride and self. Nevertheless, Jesus' warnings are clear.

- *Harshness*: If you are mean in your treatment of others, if there is an absence of gentleness in your treatment of others, take heed.
- *Grasping*: If you make sure you always get yours first, if *numero uno* is the subtle driving force in your life, if you care little about how your actions affect others, beware.
- *Vengeful*: If you are known as someone never to cross, if you always get your "pound of flesh," be on your guard.
- *Uncontrolled*: If rage fills your soul so that life is a series of explosions occasioned by the "fools" in your life, watch out.

Again, this is not to suggest that you are not a Christian if you fall into these sins, but rather to point out that if they are part of your persona, if you are a self-satisfied "Christian" who thinks that the lack of gentleness and meekness is "just you" and people will have to get used to it, if you are not repentant, you are probably not a Christian.

Jesus' words are not demanding perfection. The point is, however, that if a gentle/meek spirit is not at least imperfectly present in your life, if it is not incipient and growing, you may very well not have the smile of Christ, which is everything.

The Sublime Paradox

The reward for meekness is truly amazing: "They will inherit the earth."

As was mentioned, the inspiration for this magnificent paradox is Psalm 37, which encourages God's people not to fret because of evil, but rather to trust because "the meek will inherit the land" (v. 11; cf. vv. 9, 22, 29, 34). In the New Testament, God's people are not a physical nation—they are gathered from all nations and tongues. And the land/earth they inherit is not a physical plot of ground—it is heaven itself. The time is coming when, as fellow heirs with Christ (Romans 8:17), we will reign with Him in His earthly kingdom. We will inherit the earth. We will even judge the world (1 Corinthians 6:2). The paradox will be literally fulfilled, far beyond our wildest dreams.

But there is also a present inheritance that abundantly enriches our earthly existence. There is a sense in which those who set their minds on riches never possess anything. This was given classic expression by one of the world's wealthiest men when asked how much is enough money. "Just a little bit more," he answered. He owned everything, yet possessed nothing!

It is the meek who own the earth now, for when their life is free from the tyranny of "just a little more," when a gentle spirit caresses their approach to their rights, then they possess all. As Izaak Walton explained:

48

I could there sit quietly, and looking on the waters see fishes leaping at flies of several shapes and colors. Looking on the hills, I could behold them spotted with woods and groves. Looking down the meadows, I could see a boy gathering lilies and lady-smocks, and there a girl cropping columbines and cowslips, all to make garlands suitable to this present month of May. As I thus sat, joying in mine own happy condition, I did thankfully remember what my Saviour said, that the meek possess the earth.[6]

The meek are the only ones who inherit the earth. The "they" in "they shall inherit" is emphatic: *they alone, only they,* shall inherit the earth. They are rich right now; and fifty billion trillion years into eternity they will be lavishing in the unfolding of "the incomparable riches of his grace" (Ephesians 2:7).

Becoming Meek

There are three concurrent paths to Christlike meekness.

First, we must realize that a gentle, caressing spirit is a gift of the Holy Spirit (Galatians 5:23). Therefore, it comes only through grace. We must cast ourselves on God, asking in humble prayer that He give us life, make us His children, and instill in us a spirit of meekness. At the same time, we can ask confidently because we know that if we ask anything according to His will He will do it (cf. John 14:13; 1 John 5:14). Such asking ought to be continual because every soul needs to grow in grace regardless of one's level of spiritual maturity.

Second, we must yoke ourselves to Jesus, for He was the incarnation of meekness. Our Lord said of Himself, "Take my yoke upon you and learn from me, for I am gentle and humble in heart, and you will find rest for your souls. For my yoke is easy and my burden is light" (Matthew 11:29-30). Jesus promises us that if we yoke ourselves to Him, we will learn gentleness and humility.

In biblical times a young ox was yoked to an older, experienced ox so that the older might train him to perform properly. By bearing the same yoke, the untrained ox learned the proper pace and how to heed the direction of the master. We learn by being yoked to Christ, as we surrender our lives to Him for direction.

Third, we must give close attention to the progression of thought in the Beatitudes, for it provides us with a three-step ladder to meekness. The initial step begins in the first Beatitude (Matthew 5:3) with poverty of spirit, which comes from a true knowledge of ourselves. We realize that there is nothing within us that would commend us to God. We fall short. We need God.

In the next Beatitude (v. 4) we progress to mourning. We most naturally lament our state of spiritual poverty. This mourning is an enviable state because in it we are blessed and comforted.

We should note that poverty of spirit and mourning are negative. However, when true poverty of spirit and spiritual mourning are present, they make way for the positive virtue of meekness. In a sense, meekness is superior to the two preceding states because it grows out of them. The process is all so natural, so beautiful, and yet also quite supernatural!

We must stop here and say to ourselves, "I see how the progression works, and I see that it comes by grace, but how can I know when I am truly meek?" That is a good question. Martyn Lloyd-Jones gave his congregation in Westminster Chapel the answer, and I can say it no better. "The man who is truly meek is the man who is amazed that God and man can think of him as well as they do and treat him as well as they do."[7] The test as to whether we are truly meek is not whether we can say we *are* poor sinners, but rather what we *do* when someone else calls us vile sinners. Try it!

The Need for Gentle Christians

We need to rise above superficial Christianity. None of us must imagine that because we have good manners and display the proper social conventions we are fulfilling the meekness called for in this third Beatitude.

·Evangelical passwords and civilities are not enough. God will not be impressed, nor will the world. May the paradoxes of the Sermon on the Mount penetrate our beings and drive us to an ongoing poverty of spirit, ongoing mourning, and ongoing meekness.

We cannot afford *not* to have this happen! Those closest to us need to see positive spiritual reality in our lives, especially the paradox of Christian meekness. They need to see its strength, as we are willing to put our lives on the line for others and to stand tall for truth when necessary. They need to see gentleness and a non-retaliatory spirit within us. And when they do, they will see Jesus. That is who the world really needs to see!

CHAPTER FIVE

THE FULLNESS OF HUNGER

"Blessed are those who hunger and thirst
for righteousness, for they will be filled."

(MATTHEW 5:6)

Nutritionists have dramatized the importance of diet by telling us that we are what we eat. The thinking is, if we eat too many doughnuts and cream puffs, we'll become walking pastries. And the argument is pretty sound, as far as it goes.

In the realm of the mind and the spirit, "you are what you eat" is more penetrating. If you feed on violence, excitement, erotica, and materialism, you will eventually personify them. You will become what you eat.

I think we can accurately say that Elvis Presley never understood this. His life was a pitiful pursuit of materialism and sensuality. In Elvis's heyday he earned between $5 million and $6 million a year. It is estimated that he grossed $100 million in his first two years of stardom.

He had three jets, two Cadillacs, a Rolls-Royce, a Lincoln Continental, Buick and Chrysler station wagons, a Jeep, a dune buggy, a converted bus, and three motorcycles.

His favorite car was his 1960 Cadillac limousine. The top was covered with pearl-white Naugahyde. The body was sprayed with forty coats of a specially prepared paint that included crushed diamonds and fish scales. Nearly all the metal trim was plated with eighteen-karat gold.

Inside the car there were two gold-flake telephones, a gold vanity case containing a gold electric razor and gold hair clippers, an electric shoe buffer, a gold-plated television, a record player, an amplifier, air conditioning, and a refrigerator that was capable of making ice in two minutes. He had everything.

Elvis's sensuality is legendary. Those friends and relatives most familiar with his state in the last months of his life tragically reveal that Elvis had very much become the victim of his appetites. He was what he had eaten—in the profoundest sense.

Elvis Presley's tragic life dramatizes the significance of the Lord's teaching in this fourth Beatitude, because in it Jesus sets forth the appetite and menu that bring spiritual well-being: "Blessed are those who hunger and thirst for righteousness, for they will be filled."

In this splendidly paradoxical sentence Jesus tells us what we ought to eat and how we must eat if we are to have spiritual health and ultimate satisfaction. Spiritual health comes from hunger.

A Healthy Hunger

Because Christ declares that hunger for righteousness is essential to spiritual health and satisfaction, we must carefully consider what it means. Some have supposed that it is the *objective righteousness* described in Romans that God reckons to the believer's account, sometimes called imputed righteousness—"righteousness from God" (Romans 1:17; 3:21-22; cf. Philippians 3:9). However, while the gift of such righteousness is foundational to every believer's salvation, that is not what is meant here.

Others have confined the meaning to *social righteousness*, the righteous treatment of the poor and oppressed. This is certainly part of the meaning because in the preceding context (4:12-17) Matthew quotes Isaiah 9:1-2, which goes on to describe the social justice that will result from the coming of Messiah's reign. However, the root meaning here is determined by the seven occurrences of "righteousness" in the Sermon on the Mount that indicate it means a *subjective righteousness*, an inner righteousness that works itself out in one's living in conformity to God's will—righteous living. Thus, those who "hunger and thirst for righteousness" long to live righteously, and for righteousness to prevail in the world. It is a passionate desire, which begins with one's own life, that all things should be lived in line with God's will.

This desire to live in compliance with God's will is expansive. It includes an increasing sense of a need for God—to be like Him. To hunger and thirst for this righteousness means longing after the practical righteousness that the Beatitudes represent both personally and in the world. The one who hungers and thirsts wants the character of the kingdom. He pants after the fruit of the Spirit. He wants God's will and all it entails.

A Desperate Hungering

The fourth Beatitude is a call to pursue conformity to God's will stated in the most extreme of terms. The intensity of the expression is difficult for us to feel because if we are thirsty today, all we need to do is turn on the tap for cold, refreshing water; or if we are hungry, we just open the refrigerator. However, to the ancient Palestinian the expression was terribly alive because he was never far from the possibility of dehydration or starvation.

It is not a comfortable picture. Jesus is far from recommending a genteel desire for spiritual nourishment, but rather a starvation for righteousness, a desperate hungering to be conformed to God's will.

The Beatitude is further intensified by the fact that this hungering is continual. "Blessed are those who are hungering and thirsting for righteousness." King David, at his best, was like this. He walked with God as few mortals have. He penned some of our favorite Psalms about his lofty spiritual experiences. And at the same time he wrote of his continual thirst and hunger: "O God, you are my God, earnestly I seek you; my soul thirsts for you, my body longs for you, in a dry and weary land where there is no water" (Psalm 63:1). "And I—in righteousness I will see your face; when I awake, I will be satisfied with seeing your likeness" (Psalm 17:15).

This is the way it is for a healthy believer. He or she never has enough of God and righteousness. He or she is always hungry.

Such Hungering Either Repulses or Draws Us

The language of this Beatitude does not make sense to the modern ear. Indeed, it is too strong for some Christians. It rules out sleek, self-satisfied, halfhearted religion. In fact, hungering and thirsting for righteousness is the only approach the Beatitude accepts.

For some, Jesus' pronouncement may uncover buried, almost forgotten glimmers of past life when you first came to Christ and perpetually hungered and thirsted for righteousness. You couldn't get enough of Jesus or His Word. You were joyously desperate for the things of God. You also cared about the world and its spiritual famine. You welcomed opportunities for self-sacrifice and were willing to go for it all. But time blunted your desires, "the realities of life" took over, and that delectable hunger ceased. Now you are content with a life of lesser, limited devotion.

Yet you have not quite forgotten the joy and warmth of earlier times, and Jesus' words here still stir you. If so, you should heed His call, because you can be restored to what you were meant to be.

You must never be spiritually satisfied. You must pray that

each decade of your life will find you more thirsty for a life pleasing to God.

"Blessed are those who desperately hunger and thirst for righteousness," says our Lord.

Hungering People Know Christ

Jesus pronounces the spiritually famished to be "blessed" or approved. The reason is this: those who truly hunger and thirst know Christ. And that is why this is such a penetrating warning to evangelicals. Concern for righteous living is on the decline in the evangelical church. Many watch more murders and adulteries on television in one week than their grandparents read about in a lifetime—and with no twinge of conscience. Their casual viewing is a tacit approval of evil. The pollsters tell us that the ethical gap is narrowing between the church and the world. And many evangelicals are no more concerned about the unrighteous plight of the world than their non-Christian neighbors. Some professing evangelicals would regard a desperate longing for righteousness as odd, even fanatical.

If you have no longing for righteousness, you had better initiate a careful analysis of your soul. Christ's words are such a gracious test, because each of us knows in his heart of hearts whether he really does long for righteous living.

However, if you do hunger and thirst for righteousness, if the Lord has given you a holy discontent with your life, you have His smile!

A Hungerer's Reward

This Beatitude is, of course, another attention-grabbing paradox. It suggests that those who continually hunger are satisfied. Yet, how can one be hungry and satisfied at the same time? Or how can one be satisfied and experience hunger? Satisfied, but never satisfied? Full, yet empty? Content, but discontent?

Paradoxical Satisfaction

How does it work? Like this. Someone left a plate of brownies in the office. I resisted temptation (for a minute or two!) and then poured myself a cup of coffee and retreated to my study, brownie in hand. When I bit in, I tasted the best of brownies, for it was layered with caramel. I was "in heaven" with my brownie and cup of coffee. And I was completely satisfied—for about half an hour. Then I began to hunger and thirst for more! And I ate again with the same effect. It was a sublime cycle.

There you have the idea. The paradox describes a spiritual cycle. The more one conforms to God's will, the more fulfilled and content one becomes. But that in turn spawns a greater discontent. Our hunger increases and intensifies in the very act of being satisfied.

Paul lived in the blessing of this paradox. He wrote to Timothy, "I know whom I have believed" (2 Timothy 1:12). Yet to the Philippians he expressed a profound longing for Christ—"to know Christ and the power of his resurrection and the fellowship of sharing in his sufferings, becoming like him in his death" (Philippians 3:10). Paul knew Christ intimately, but the intimacy and satisfaction made him long for more. Bernard of Clairvaux sang of this cycle. Read his great words slowly:

> *We taste Thee, O Thou living Bread*
> *And long to feast upon Thee still*
> *We drink of Thee, the Fountainhead,*
> *And thirst our souls from Thee to fill.*

Complete Satisfaction

The world only offers us empty cups. That is why our text emphasizes that "they alone (those who hunger and thirst) will be filled." No one can know anything of this satisfaction but a believer.

The Scriptures joyfully attest to the satisfaction that Christ brings:

> "But whoever drinks the water I give him will never thirst. Indeed, the water I give him will become in him a spring of water welling up to eternal life." (John 4:14)

> "I am the bread of life. He who comes to me will never go hungry, and he who believes in me will never be thirsty." (John 6:35)

> . . . for he satisfies the thirsty and fills the hungry with good things. (Psalm 107:9)

Eternal Satisfaction

The image of a divine feast is used more than once by Jesus to illustrate the satisfactions of the kingdom. On one occasion Jesus told His disciples, "And I confer on you a kingdom, just as my Father conferred one on me, so that you may eat and drink at my table in my kingdom" (Luke 22:29-30). Now that will be eternal satisfaction!

We need to believe the words of Isaiah: "Come, all you who are thirsty, come to the waters; and you who have no money, come, buy and eat! Come, buy wine and milk without money and without cost. Why spend money on what is not bread, and your labor on what does not satisfy? Listen, listen to me, and eat what is good, and your soul will delight in the richest of fare" (Isaiah 55:1-2).

We need to practice Jesus' words: "But seek first his kingdom and his righteousness, and all these things will be given to you as well" (Matthew 6:33).

God's Call: A Profound Hunger

Consider the force of this fourth Beatitude as we have opened it: "Blessed are those who hunger and thirst (like the starving do for food and the thirsty do for water) for righteousness (righteous living), for they will be filled (satisfied completely)."

"You are what you eat" is not as simple as it may first appear. It is profoundly esoteric. The tragedy of our time is that the world is hungering and thirsting after sex and wealth, violence and excitement. The church's tragedy is that many in her are seeking the same thing— and their diets are making them as empty and pathetic as the world.

We must remember that Jesus has provided us with the menu and appetite. The main course is righteousness—conformity to His will. The method is desperation. We are to hunger for righteousness–and so pursue it with all that is in us. The result is profound satisfaction, now and forever.

How Is Your Appetite?

The answer lies in the spiritual logic of the Beatitudes.

- We must begin with the first Beatitude, true poverty of spirit, realizing that there is nothing within us that commends us to God. We must affirm our spiritual bankruptcy.
- Next, we must graduate to the second Beatitude, truly mourning our sins as well as the sin around us.
- Then we must ascend to the third Beatitude, by allowing our spiritual bankruptcy and mourning to instill in us a truly meek and gentle spirit.
- Finally, as we live the logic of the Beatitudes, we will be able to desperately hunger and thirst for righteousness.

There are few things more important than our spiritual appetite. We are what we eat.

Evangelicals, we need to hear Jesus' words afresh: "If you knew the gift of God and who it is that asks you for a drink, you would have asked him and he would have given you living water" (John 4:10).

CHAPTER SIX

THE DIVIDEND OF MERCY

"Blessed are the merciful,
for they will be shown mercy."

(MATTHEW 5:7)

Years ago a small-town merchant had identical twin boys who were inseparable. They were so close that they even dressed alike. It was said that their extraordinary closeness was the reason they never married. When their father died, they took over the family business. Their relationship was considered "a model of creative collaboration."

Busy, one of the brothers neglected to ring up a sale and absentmindedly left a dollar bill on top of the cash register while he went to the front of the store to wait on another customer. Remembering the dollar, he returned to deposit it only to find the bill was gone. He asked his brother if he had seen it, but the brother said he had not.

An hour later he asked his brother again, but this time with an obvious note of suspicion. His brother became angry and defensive. Every time they tried to discuss the matter, the conflict grew worse, culminating in vicious charges and countercharges. The incredible outcome was the dissolution of their partnership, the installation of a partition down the middle of the store, and two competing businesses. This continued for twenty years—an open, divisive sore in the community.

One day a car with an out-of-state license pulled up in front of the stores. A well-dressed man entered one brother's shop and asked how long the store had been there. Learning it had been twenty years, he said, "Then you are the one with whom I must settle an old score."

> Some twenty years ago I was out of work, drifting from place to place, and I happened to get off a boxcar in your town. I had absolutely no money and had not eaten for three days. As I was walking down the alley behind your store, I looked in and saw a dollar bill on the top of the cash register. Everyone else was in the front of the store. I had been raised in a Christian home and I had never before in all my life stolen anything, but that morning I was so hungry I gave in to the temptation, slipped through the door, and took that dollar bill. That act has weighed on my conscience ever since, and I finally decided that I would never be at peace until I came back and faced up to that old sin and made amends. Would you let me now replace that money and pay you whatever is appropriate for damages?[1]

When the stranger finished his confession, he was amazed to see the old store owner shaking his head in deep sorrow and beginning to weep. Finally the old man gained control and, taking the gentleman by the arm, asked him to go to the store next door and tell its owner the same story. The stranger complied. Only this time two old men who looked almost identical wept side by side.[2]

From our distance we cannot say whether the two brothers professed to be believers, or were even churchgoers. Given the time and the culture, they probably owned some religious inclinations. Indeed, they could have been enthusiastic churchmen—even evangelicals. But whatever their spiritual profession, their merciless, unforgiving spirits revealed hearts that had never understood the mercy of God. For if they had, they themselves would have been merciful.

The fifth Beatitude—"Blessed are the merciful, for they will be shown mercy"—is the perfect corrective for all those who are caught in bitterness.

If you have problems similar to the two unhappy brothers, this chapter could lead you to liberation.

The Merciful

The basic idea of the Greek word translated *merciful* is "to give help to the wretched, to relieve the miserable." Here the essential thought is that mercy gives attention to those in misery. From this we make the important distinction between mercy and grace. *Grace* is shown to the undeserving; *mercy* is compassion to the miserable. Thus the synonym for *mercy* is *compassion*. Mercy, however, is not simply *feeling* compassion. Mercy exists when something is done to alleviate distress. This is uniform in the Old Testament (cf. Hosea and Amos 5). Jesus made this perfectly clear when, after He told the Parable of the Good Samaritan, He asked His questioner:

> "Which of these three do you think was a neighbor to the man who fell into the hands of robbers?" The expert in the law replied, "The one who had mercy on him." Jesus told him, "Go and do likewise." (Luke 10:36-37)

Mercy Is Compassion in Action

We must never imagine that we are merciful because we *feel* compassionate toward someone in distress. Mercy means *active* goodwill. This was well understood by the nineteenth-century preacher who happened across a friend whose horse had just been accidentally killed. While a crowd of onlookers expressed empty words of sympathy, the preacher stepped forward and said to the loudest sympathizer, "I am sorry five pounds. How much are you sorry?" And then he passed the hat. True mercy demands action.

Mercy Is Forgiving

New Testament scholar Robert Guelich has shown that especially in this Beatitude *merciful* describes one who forgives and pardons another who is in the wrong.[3] An inspiring display of this forgiving aspect of mercy in Scripture is that of Joseph to his brothers. The only reason they had not murdered him as a boy was that as they were ready to perform the act, they saw an approaching caravan and decided to sell him into slavery instead. Years later, when Joseph had his guilty brothers literally "at his mercy," he showed them exactly that. There was *compassion* as he wept for their misery, and then *action* as he met their needs. There was *forgiveness* as he restored them all to his grace, saying, "You intended to harm me, but God intended it for good" (Genesis 50:20).

The merciful person remembers his own sin and God's mercy to him, he understands the weaknesses of others, and he forgives. W. E. Sangster, the much-loved pastor of the renowned Westminster Central Hall, London, was graced with this quality in his own life. "It was Christmas time in my home," as he tells it:

> One of my guests had come a couple of days early and saw me sending off the last of my Christmas cards. He was startled to see a certain name and address. "Surely, you are not sending a greeting card to him," he said. "Why not?" I asked. "But you remember," he began, "eighteen months ago . . ." I remembered, then, the thing the man had publicly said about me, but I remembered also resolving at the time with God's help . . . to forget. And God had "made" me forget! I posted the card.[4]

I once had an associate who was like this. On one memorable occasion the name of someone came up who had grievously slandered him, and I said something derogatory about that person. But to my embarrassment (and instruction!), my friend began to quietly defend his slanderer: "Life has been hard for him . . . we have no idea of the pressures he has been under . . . he has done a lot of good things too." My colleague had compassion on the miserable soul who had given him so much trouble and, from what I could tell, had forgiven him! How beautiful that was! Our text tells us what God thinks of this: "Blessed are the merciful." Jesus says, "Such are the ones whom I approve."

They Shall Receive Mercy

The reason the merciful are blessed is that "they will be shown mercy." The word "they" in the phrase is emphatic: "Blessed are the merciful, for they (they alone) will be shown mercy." Other Scriptures teach the same idea. James says, "Judgment without mercy will be shown to anyone who has not been merciful" (James 2:13). Jesus Himself says, "For if you forgive men when they sin against you, your heavenly Father will also forgive you. But if you do not forgive men their sins, your Father will not forgive your sins" (Matthew 6:14-15).

Predictably, some have completely missed the point here, supposing that this Beatitude teaches that one can merit God's mercy by performing acts of mercy. Such an idea is at complete variance with the rest of Scripture, which teaches salvation by grace alone (Ephesians 2:8-9). Moreover, if receiving God's forgiveness could only be merited by becoming forgiving, none of us would ever be truly forgiven, for none would ever absolutely meet this standard.

What this Beatitude means is that those who are truly God's children, and as such are objects of His mercy, will themselves be merciful and will receive mercy in the end. Showing mercy is evidence that we have received mercy.

This interpretation suggests two very penetrating tests. The first is this: if we have no mercy toward those who are physically and economically in distress, we are not Christians. Notice I did not say we become Christians by showing mercy toward the unfortunate, but that we are not believers if we are unwilling to show mercy to them. This is precisely the point of the Parable of the Good Samaritan. Jesus told the story to demonstrate that the religious establishment of His day did not fulfill the Great *Shema*—loving God with all one's might and one's neighbor as oneself (Luke 10:25-28). The fact that the priest and the Levite turned away from the needy man proved they did not love their neighbor as themselves; they thus failed to fulfill the Law and were lost. But the Samaritan's act of mercy showed that he loved his neighbor as himself, and that he was living within the gracious parameters of the Law. He was a lover of God and man.

If we remain impassive or callous to human need and refuse to do anything about it, we need to take a good long look at ourselves and see if we really are believers. John says it best: "If anyone has material possessions and sees his brother in need but has no pity on him, how can the love of God be in him?" (1 John 3:17). This is a test evangelicals haven't liked. Today, I suspect, there are some who would reject this test outright. If so, they are in great peril of soul. True belief is never to be divorced from attitude and action.

The second test involves the corresponding aspect of mercy—forgiveness. The test is this: if we refuse to exercise mercy by extending forgiveness, we are not Christians. Of course, it is frightening to maintain that we cannot be truly forgiven unless we have forgiving spirits. But it is true, because when God's grace comes into our hearts it makes us merciful. Forgiveness demonstrates whether we have been forgiven. So the telling line is this: if we refuse to be merciful, there is only one reason—we have never understood the grace of Christ. We are outside grace and are unforgiven.

Jesus taught this in the Parable of the Unmerciful Slave (Matthew 18:21-35). The slave owed his master an immense sum—in today's currency about twenty million dollars. The debt was impossible to repay, so he pleaded with his master who, with astonishing compassion, forgave him the entire debt. Incredibly, however, the wicked slave went out, found one of his fellow slaves who owed him 2,000 dollars, and threw him in prison. When the other slaves reported this injustice to their master, he summoned the wicked slave:

> "'You wicked servant,' he said, 'I canceled all that debt of yours because you begged me to. Shouldn't you have had mercy on your fellow servant just as I had on you?' In anger his master turned him over to the jailers to be tortured, until he should pay back all he owed. This is how my heavenly Father will treat each of you unless you forgive your brother from your heart." (Matthew 18:32-35)

These are hard, violent, surgical words. But they are mercifully so. The Lord here warns the religious person who attends church, can recite the appropriate answers, leads an outwardly moral life, but holds a death grip on his grudges. Jesus warns the one who will not forgive his relatives or his former business associates regardless of their pleas. He warns the one who nourishes hatreds, cherishes animosities, and otherwise lives in settled malice.

Such a person had better take stock of his life.

Some words of qualification are in order. The warning is not for those who find that bitterness and hatred recur even though they have forgiven the offender. The fact that you have forgiven and continue to forgive is a sign of grace, despite the ambivalences and imperfections of your forgiveness. The warning is for those who have no desire to forgive. Their souls are in danger.

There may also be some who find forgiveness difficult because they have been recently offended and are still in such emotional shock that they *cannot* properly respond. The warning is not for these.

The overall lesson is, if we are Christians, we can forgive and will forgive, however imperfectly it may be. We cannot live like the miserable brothers who divided over a dollar bill.

On Forgiving

The late Corrie ten Boom recalled in her book *The Hiding Place* a postwar meeting with a guard from the Ravensbruck concentration camp, where her sister had died and she herself had been subjected to horrible indignities.

It was at a church service in Munich that I saw him, the former S.S. man who had stood guard at the shower room door in the processing center at Ravensbruck. He was the first of our actual jailers that I had seen since that time. And suddenly it was all there—the roomful of mocking men, the heaps of clothing, Betsie's pain-blanched face.

He came up to me as the church was emptying, beaming and bowing. "How grateful I am for your message, Fraulein," he said. "To think that, as you say, He has washed my sins away!"

His hand was thrust out to shake mine. And I, who had preached so often to the people in Bloemendaal the need to forgive, kept my hand at my side.

Even as the angry, vengeful thoughts boiled through me, I saw the sin of them. Jesus Christ had died for this man; was I going to ask for more? Lord Jesus, I prayed, forgive me and help me to forgive him.

I tried to smile, I struggled to raise my hand. I could not. I felt nothing, not the slightest spark of warmth or charity. And so again I breathed a silent prayer. Jesus, I cannot forgive him. Give me Your forgiveness.

As I took his hand the most incredible thing happened. From my shoulder along my arm and through my hand a current seemed to pass from me to him, while into my heart sprang a love for this stranger that almost overwhelmed me.[5]

Forgiveness is possible for the most grievous of wounds. When I was a young man, I was acquainted with a Christian who took in a troubled teenager and tried to help him. The boy brutally murdered this man's daughter. Amazingly, my friend visited him in prison, forgave him, and eventually led him to Christ.

If you are a Christian, regardless of the wrong done to you, you can forgive. By God's grace, you can forgive the domestic wrong. By God's grace, you can forgive the professional wrong. For your soul's sake, you must.

When we began our study of the Beatitudes we observed that they were given to us so that we could ascertain two things: first, the authenticity of our faith, and second, the health of our spiritual lives. In the searchlight of this Beatitude, "Blessed are the merciful, for they will be shown mercy," is your salvation authentic? Are you merciful? Are you forgiving? Or do you hold grudges as your treasured possessions?

If you have come to understand that you are without grace and mercy, then no more fitting word could be commended to you here than this parable:

> "Two men went up to the temple to pray, one a Pharisee and the other a tax collector. The Pharisee stood up and prayed about himself: 'God, I thank you that I am not like other men—robbers, evildoers, adulterers—or even like this tax collector. I fast twice a week and give a tenth of all I get.' But the tax collector stood at a distance. He would not even look up to heaven, but beat his breast and said, 'God, have mercy on me, a sinner.' I tell you that this man, rather than the other, went home justified

before God. For everyone who exalts himself will be humbled, and he who humbles himself will be exalted." (Luke 18:10-14)

Now do as the sinner did. Confess your sin. Affirm your faith in Christ as your only hope of salvation. Rest in His mercy. Thank Him for saving you.

If you need to develop the compassion and forgiveness of a merciful spirit, here are some suggestions:

- *Confession*: Admit your need to God. Pray to this effect: "Father, I know Your mercy. I have been merciful at times. But, God, I need more compassion, and I need to forgive. I know this is Your will for me. Help me."
- *Scripture*: Read the Scriptures that have to do with mercy and compassion. Begin with Hosea 6:6, and then read Jesus' application of it in Matthew 9:9-13 and 23:23. Also examine Micah 6:8 and Amos 5:21-24. And especially meditate on Luke 10:30-37. Regarding forgiveness, read Matthew 6:14-15 and 18:21-35.
- *Mercy*: Then get out and do mercy. Volitionally forgive those who have wronged you. Purposely become involved with those who are hurting.

Enjoy God's smile! "Blessed are the merciful, for they will be shown mercy."

CHAPTER SEVEN

THE REWARD OF PURITY

"Blessed are the pure in heart,
for they will see God."

(MATTHEW 5:8)

In 1982 the *Los Angeles Times* carried the story of Anna Mae Pennica, a sixty-two-year-old woman who had been blind from birth.[1] At age forty-seven she married a man she met in a Braille class; and for the first fifteen years of their marriage he did the seeing for both of them until he completely lost his vision to retinitis pigmentosa. Mrs. Pennica had never seen the green of spring or the blue of a winter sky. Yet because she had grown up in a loving, supportive family, she never felt resentful about her handicap and always exuded a remarkably cheerful spirit.

Then in October 1981 Dr. Thomas Pettit of the Jules Stein Eye Institute of the University of California at Los Angeles performed surgery to remove the rare congenital cataracts from the lens of her left eye—and Mrs. Pennica saw for the first time ever! The newspaper account does not record her initial response, but it does tell us that she found that everything was "so much bigger and brighter" than she ever imagined. While she immediately recognized her husband and others she had known well, other acquaintances were taller or shorter, heavier or skinnier than she had pictured them.

Since that day Mrs. Pennica has hardly been able to wait to wake up in the morning, splash her eyes with water, put on her glasses, and enjoy the changing morning light. Her vision is almost 20/30—good enough to pass a driver's test.

Think how wonderful it must have been for Anna Mae Pennica when she looked for the first time at the faces she had only felt, or when she saw the kaleidoscope of a Pacific sunset or a tree waving its branches or a bird in flight. The gift of physical sight is wonderful. And the miracle of seeing for the first time can hardly be described.

A Greater Seeing

Yet there is a seeing that surpasses even this—and that is seeing God. Since nothing is higher than God, seeing God is logically the greatest joy one can experience. Thus, when we pass from this world and see the face of Christ, the joy of that first split second will transcend all the accumulated joys of life. It will be the highest good, the *summum bonum*, the greatest joy, beside which the wonderful story of Mrs. Pennica's "miracle" fades in comparison.

This is what the sixth Beatitude is about—seeing God. "Blessed are the pure in heart, for they will see God." Jesus' words tell us how to get 20/20 spiritual vision. If we want to see God, this is *the* great text.

The Beatitude: "Blessed Are the Pure in Heart"

As we begin, we must determine what "pure" means. Its Old Testament usage tells us that it refers to internal cleansing. Very likely Jesus' reference to "pure in heart" comes from the famous rhetorical answer to the questions of Psalm 24:3-4: "Who may ascend the hill of the LORD? Who may stand in his holy place? He who has clean hands and a pure heart." Significantly, the Old Testament prophets looked forward to the time when God would give the people clean hearts. Ezekiel records God's words:

> "I will sprinkle clean water on you, and you will be clean; I will cleanse you from all your impurities and from all your idols. I will give you a new heart and put a new spirit in you; I will remove from you your heart of stone and give you a heart of flesh." (36:25-26)

Jeremiah similarly envisaged a new covenant in which God would put His "law in their minds and write it on their hearts" (31:33).

In Jesus' day the need was urgent because of the Pharisees' externalizing. Hence Jesus' warning:

> "Woe to you, teachers of the law and Pharisees, you hypocrites! You clean the outside of the cup and dish, but inside they are full of greed and self-indulgence. Blind Pharisee! First clean the inside of the cup and dish, and then the outside also will be clean. Woe to you, teachers of the law and Pharisees, you hypocrites! You are like whitewashed tombs, which look beautiful on the outside but on the inside are full of dead men's bones and everything unclean. In the same way, on the outside you appear to people as righteous but on the inside you are full of hypocrisy and wickedness." (Matthew 23:25-28)

The Pharisees could well be characterized as saying, "Blessed are the outwardly clean, for they shall see God." So we see the necessity for the sixth Beatitude's call for a radical inner purity: "Blessed are the pure in heart, for they will see God."

In addition to this primary meaning, "pure" also calls for a purity of devotion. William Barclay tells us that the Greek word was used to describe clear water, sometimes metals without alloy, sometimes grain that had been winnowed, and sometimes feelings that are unmixed.[2] As it is used in our text, it carries the idea of being free from every taint of evil.

We must keep this squarely in mind because it is normally supposed that "pure" as in "pure in heart" primarily refers to being pure in mind regarding matters of sensuality. It certainly includes these matters. But the idea cannot be so limited, for it goes far deeper. Here in the sixth Beatitude it means a heart that does not bring mixed motives and divided loyalties to its relationship with God. It is a heart of singleness in devotion to God—pure, unmixed devotion. James refers to this idea when he says, "Purify your hearts, you double-minded" (James 4:8). That is, "Get rid of your mixed motives, your duplicity, your doublemindedness; be simple and pure in your devotion. (Cf. the commendations for an "undivided heart" in Psalm 86:11, Jeremiah 32:39, Ezekiel 11:19, 1 Corinthians 7:35.)

Negatively, we can imagine this idea from everyday life if we reflect on those people who, having been introduced to us, keep talking and smiling, while at the same time looking behind and around us at other people and things. They really are not interested in us; they only see us as objects or a means to an end. In the God-man relationship such behavior is scandalous. Positively stated then, "pure" is represented by the words *focus, absorption, concentration, sincerity,* and *singleness.*

"Blessed are the pure" is a searching statement, because focusing on God with a singleness of heart is one of the biggest challenges to twentieth-century Christians. Very few in this frenetic age are capable of the spiritual attention this Beatitude calls for.

Depth of Devotion

The depth of what is called for here is seen in the qualifying words "in heart." We are to be singly focused in heart on God. In the Bible, *heart* means more than just the mind; it also includes the emotions, and the will. It is the totality of our ability to think, feel, and decide. So "pure in heart" means that not only our minds but our feelings and actions are to be concentrated singly on God. If our focus is merely intellectual, we are not pure in heart. As Martyn Lloyd-Jones paraphrases it, "Blessed are those who are pure, not only on the surface but in the center of their being and at the source of every activity."[3] This is a daunting requirement—a radical cleanness of heart, totally focused on God.

The depth of this heart requirement is further underlined by the realization that it is from the heart that all our human problems come. Jeremiah said, "The heart is deceitful above all things and beyond cure" (Jeremiah 17:9). Jesus said, "For out of the heart come evil thoughts, murder, adultery, sexual immorality, theft, false testimony, slander" (Matthew 15:19). Again He said, "Nothing outside a man can make him 'unclean' by going into him. Rather, it is what comes out of a man that makes him 'unclean.' For from within, out of men's hearts, come evil thoughts" (Mark 7:15, 21). The Scriptures are conclusive. But our hearts tell us the same. All we have to do is look into our own hearts of darkness, observing the mixed motives, the distractions, the divided loyalties, to know this is perfectly true. The dictum of Ivan Turgenev, the nineteenth-century Russian novelist, speaks for us all:

> *I do not know what the heart*
> *of a bad man is like.*
> *But I do know what the heart*
> *of a good man is like.*
> *And*
> *it is terrible.*

An Impossible Depth

The looming question is, therefore, how can we ever accomplish this? This Beatitude is beyond our reach. Jesus is asking for perfection. And at the end of the first section of the Sermon on the Mount, this is precisely what He says: "Be perfect, therefore, as your heavenly Father is perfect" (Matthew 5:48). This drives us to despair, for none of us *perfectly* models any of the Beatitudes. None of us perfectly exhibits a poverty of spirit. None of us perfectly mourns our sins. None of us is perfectly humble and gentle. None of us perfectly thirsts. No one is perfectly pure in heart.

Then what are we to do? There is only one answer. We must cast ourselves on the grace of God and thus receive His radical renewal. We must ask Him to implant and nourish the character of the kingdom in our lives. If we do this, these qualities will take root and grow within us, though we will never attain absolute perfection in this life.

If the character of the kingdom is not present, then we must question whether we are truly believers. Here, with the sixth Beatitude—"Blessed (approved) are the pure in heart"—we must ask ourselves, "Is my heart clean, and do I know anything of single-hearted devotion to God?" The answers to these searching questions may indicate the authenticity of our faith or, if we are believers, the state of our spiritual health.

God demands a humanly impossible character, and then gives us that character by His grace. And with that He bestows a humanly impossible vision.

The Boon: "For They Will See God"

The Beatitude's sublime benefit is a vision of God Himself. Here, as in the preceding Beatitudes, the word "they" is emphatic: "for they (they alone) will see God." And as with the other Beatitudes, the future is in immediate reference to what goes before. They will see God as they become pure in heart. And the seeing is continuous.

What this means is that it is possible to actually see God in this life—now. I think this is what blind and deaf Helen Keller meant when someone bluntly said to her, "Isn't it terrible to be blind?" To which she responded, "Better to be blind and see with your heart, than to have two good eyes and see nothing." Perhaps if it were possible for her to have heard of Mrs. Pennica's miraculous operation, she would have said, "That is wonderful. But there is yet a better seeing."

Seeing God Now

Christians see God now. Of course, they do not see Him in His total being, because that would be too much for them. However, they do see Him in many ways. That has been my experience. Before I became a Christian I won a Bible-reading contest, but the words meant nothing to me. Just a short time later when I met Christ, the Word of God came alive. I couldn't get enough. I even read at night with my flashlight! The Bible was living, and I saw God in its pages.

Believers also see and celebrate God in creation. Psalm 29 records that David watched a thunderstorm and saw God. Of thunder he says, "The voice of the LORD is over the waters; the God of glory thunders, the LORD thunders over the mighty waters. The voice of the LORD is powerful; the voice of the LORD is majestic" (vv. 3-4). When David saw the lightning his response was, "The voice of the LORD strikes with flashes of lightning" (v. 7). This kind of seeing is the special possession of the believer. We see the footprints and the hand of God in nature.

Those of faith also see Him in the events of life—even difficulties. Job exclaimed after his varied experiences of life, "My ears had heard of you but now my eyes have seen you" (Job 42:5).

Seeing More of God

The sixth Beatitude tells us that the purer our hearts become, the more we will see of God in this life. The more our hearts are focused on God, absorbed with Him, concentrated on His being, freed from distractions, sincere—*single*, the more we will see Him. As our hearts become purer, the more the Word lives and the more creation speaks. Even the adverse circumstances of life seem to sharpen our vision of God.

Seeing God in this life is the *summum bonum*—*the* highest good, because those who see Him become more and more like Him. "And we, who with unveiled faces all reflect the Lord's glory, are being transformed into his likeness with ever-increasing glory, which comes from the Lord, who is the Spirit" (2 Corinthians 3:18).

Ultimate Seeing

But there is even more to seeing God, for the "pure in heart" will one day see Him face to face. As we have said, in that split second of recognition believers will experience more joy than the sum total of accumulated joys of a long life. They will behold the dazzling blaze of His being that has been, and will always be, the abiding fascination of angels. Scripture and reason demand that we understand that it will be the greatest event of our eternal existence—the *visio Dei*, the vision of God. We need to believe it! We need the faith and vision of Job who said, "I know that my Redeemer lives, and that in the end he will stand upon the earth. And after my skin has been destroyed, yet in my flesh I will see God; I myself will see him with my own eyes—I, and not another. How my heart yearns within me!" (Job 19:25-27). Fainting hearts should be our reaction at the prospect of the vision of God.

Now think of the complete Beatitude: "Blessed (approved of God) are the pure in heart (those with a clean, unmixed heart for God), for they shall (continuously) see God (in life and in eternity)." Have we experienced, do we know, a purity of heart, an unmixed devotion to God? This is not to suggest that this is our perfect experience at every moment. But rather, do we *ever* experience it? Moreover, is this singleness our desire? If not, listen closely, for the answer exists.

On Receiving Sight

The irony of Mrs. Pennica's "miracle," according to Dr. Pettit, was that "surgical techniques available as far back as the 1940s could have corrected her problem." Mrs. Pennica lived forty of her sixty-two sightless years needlessly blind!

Now hear this, and hear it well: the "technique" for curing spiritual blindness has existed for two millennia. The procedure is radical and 100% effective, because God is the physician. You must be born again. To be pure in heart, you must be given a new heart.

When Jesus informed Nicodemus of this necessity, Nicodemus quite naturally questioned how it could be. Jesus answered, "Flesh gives birth to flesh, but the Spirit gives birth to spirit" (John 3:6), saying in effect, "That which is animal is animal, that which is vegetable is vegetable, and that which is of the Spirit is spirit. Nicodemus, it is radical indeed." Jesus explained how spiritual birth happens in these words: "You should not be surprised at my saying, 'You must be born again.' The wind blows wherever it pleases. You hear its sound, but you cannot tell where it comes from or where it is going. So it is with everyone born of the Spirit" (John 3:7-8). That is to say, "Nicodemus, it is the work of the Holy Spirit. You do not see His work, just as you do not see the wind, but only its effects." To us He says, "Trust God's Word, believe that Jesus' death on the cross paid the penalty for your sins, and thereby receive a new, pure heart in place of your heart of darkness." It is a miracle. It is all of God. It is free. It is yours as you believe.

Do you believe?

On Improving Vision

For those of us who are Christians, this text is also an opportunity to develop and enhance the purity and focus of our hearts.

First, *be absolutely honest with God about your heart's condition.* Is your heart inwardly clean? And more, is it pure in its focus on God? Ask the Holy Spirit to show you the exact state of your heart.

Second, *acknowledge that only God can make your heart pure.* This is not to suggest passivity. Paul tells us, "Therefore, my dear friends, as you have always obeyed —not only in my presence, but now much more in my absence—continue to work out your salvation with fear and trembling, for it is God who works in you to will and to act according to his good purpose" (Philippians 2:12-13). James says, "Come near to God and he will come near to you. Wash your hands, you sinners, and purify your hearts, you double-minded" (James 4:8). The biblical balance is: I must do everything I can and still realize that it is not enough; only God can make my heart pure (cf. Romans 11:6 and Ephesians 2:7a).

Third, *fill yourself with God's Word.* In the Upper Room Jesus told His disciples, "You are already clean because of the word I have spoken to you" (John 15:3). Immersion and interaction with God's Word will purify.

Fourth, *think about what you will be in eternity.* Make that hope a prominent aspect of your meditation. The Apostle John is very exact in explaining what such a hope will do to us:

> Dear friends, now we are children of God, and what we will be has not yet been made known. But we know that when he appears, we shall be like him, for we shall see him as he is. Everyone who has this hope in him purifies himself, just as he is pure. (1 John 3:2-3)

You and I are going to be transformed at the *visio Dei* into the likeness of Christ. This is the most stupendous thing we could ever be told! This is our purifying hope.

Hear Paul's charge to look for that day:

> For the grace of God that brings salvation has appeared to all men. It teaches us to say "No" to ungodliness and worldly passions, and to live self-controlled, upright and godly lives in this present age, while we wait for the blessed hope—the glorious appearing of our great God and Savior, Jesus Christ, who gave himself for us to redeem us from all wickedness and to purify for himself a people that are his very own, eager to do what is good. (Titus 2:11-14)

CHAPTER EIGHT

THE PATERNITY OF PEACE

"Blessed are the peacemakers,
for they will be called sons of God."

(MATTHEW 5:9)

The celebrated historians Will and Ariel Durant, in their book *The Lessons of History*, begin the chapter on "History and War" with these words: "War is one of the constants of history, and has not diminished with civilization and democracy. In the last 3,421 years of recorded history only 268 have seen no war."[1] That is a chilling statement. And it would, no doubt, be even more so if the facts of *unrecorded* history could be known.

War is the constant reality of life. Today anyone old enough to understand what is being said on television knows that multiple wars are being fought at this very moment. The proposed solutions are many. Some are tongue-in-cheek, like the despairing scenario which the Durants put in the mouth of a fictitious general:

> States will unite in basic cooperation only when they are in common attacked from without. Perhaps . . . we may make contact with ambitious species on other planets or stars; soon there-

after there will be interplanetary war. Then, and only then, will we of this earth be one.[2]

Seriously, some do argue the necessity that one of the super-powers gain ascendancy over the rest (through battle no doubt!) and then war will be outlawed—a *Pax Romana* revived. Others hold that the inhabitants of the world simply must come to the conclusion that war is unprofitable and refuse to fight. Do you remember the old bumper sticker, "What if they had a war and nobody came?" Another suggestion, akin to this but more elevated, is that nations must challenge the evil precedents of history and live by the Golden Rule, as legend says a Buddhist king once did.

This last idea touches on the solution, but it doesn't go far enough. The answer to war is not simply a matter of bootstrap ethics; it is profoundly theological. What is needed is a radical change in the human race if there is to be peace. No one can live the Golden Rule by mere human will. No one can master even one of the Beatitudes in his own strength. Peace is impossible for humans qua humans.

Thus the grand relevance of the seventh Beatitude: "Blessed are the peacemakers, for they will be called sons of God." This divine pronouncement, understood, taken to heart, and applied by the Holy Spirit, can not only bring inner peace to our troubled hearts but also make us instruments of peace—peacemakers. It has the potential to give us peace within and to make us mediators of peace in the lives of those around us and in society at large.

"Blessed Are the Peacemakers"

Fundamental to understanding what Christ is saying is the precise meaning of the exquisite word "peacemakers." Taking the first half of the word, *peace*, we understand it to mean much the same as the Hebrew word *shalom*, which bears the idea of wholeness and over-all well-being. When a Jew said, "Shalom," he was wishing another more than the absence of trouble, but all that made for a complete, whole life. God's peace is not narrowly defined. It is much more than the absence of strife; it encompasses all of the person—it is positive.

The second half of the word, *makers*, demands that we understand that the person is not passive but is a source of peace. As it is used here, it is a dynamic word bursting with energy. Both parts of the word "peacemakers," taken together, describe one who actively pursues peace in its fullness. He pursues more than the absence of conflict; he pursues wholeness and well-being.

Bearing this in mind, we can then understand what a peacemaker is not. A peacemaker is not, as is commonly supposed, the kind of person who is easygoing and *laissez-faire*, who doesn't care what anyone else does as long as it doesn't directly affect him. Neither is the peacemaker always tolerant—"you do your thing and I'll do mine." Nor is the peacemaker an appeaser—the kind who wants "peace at any price." Appeasement doesn't make for peace. It just puts off the conflict. The history of Europe during the 1930s is the classic example of this.

The true peacemaker, contrary to what most people think, is not afraid of making waves.

What a Peacemaker Is

What then is a peacemaker like? To begin with, he is characterized by *honesty*. If there is a problem, he admits it. The prophet Ezekiel warned against those who act as if all is well when it is not, who say "'Peace,' when there is no peace" (13:10). Such, according to Ezekiel, are merely plastering over cracked walls. The plaster obscures the cracks, but when the rain comes, the true state of the walls is revealed and the walls crumble (vv. 10-11). Jeremiah, employing similar phrasing, put it memorably: "They dress the wound of my people as though it were not serious. 'Peace, peace,' they say, when there is no peace" (Jeremiah 6:14). The peacemaker doesn't do this. He is painfully honest about the true status of relationships in the world, in the society in which he moves, and in his own personal dealings. He admits failed relationships. He admits that he is at odds with others if it is so. He honestly acknowledges tension if others have something against him. He does not pretend. He refuses to say, "Peace, peace!" when there is no peace.

How this speaks to real life. We tend to putty over the cracks. This is particularly a male tendency. Even in our most intimate relationships, men tend to act as if everything is OK when it is not. Men often avoid reality because they want peace. But their avoidance heals the wound only slightly and prepares the way for greater trouble.

Next, a peacemaker is willing to *risk pain*. Any time we attempt to bring peace personally or societally, we necessarily risk misunderstanding and failure. If we have been wrong, there is the pain of apologizing. On the other hand, we may have to shoulder the equally difficult pain of rebuking another. In any case, the peacemaker has to be willing to "risk it." The temptation is to let things slide. It is so easy to rationalize that trying to bring true peace will "only make things worse."

These two qualities of the peacemaker—honesty about the true status of peace and a willingness to risk pain in pursuing peace—beautifully anticipate the next quality, which is a paradox: *the peacemaker is a fighter*. He makes trouble to make peace. He wages peace.

God's Word enjoins such peacemaking, telling us to "make every effort to keep the unity of the Spirit through the bond of peace" (Ephesians 4:3) and to "make every effort to do what leads to peace and to mutual edification" (Romans 14:19). "If it is possible, as far as it depends on you, live at peace with everyone" (Romans 12:18). St. Francis of Assisi understood this call to the active pursuit of peace:

Lord, make me an instrument of Thy peace.
Where there is hate, may I bring love;
Where offense, may I bring pardon;
May I bring union in place of discord.

That the peacemaker is a fighter in no way justifies a verbal "license to kill." He should never be thoughtless or pugnacious. Rather his personality must be permeated with the *shalom* of God. He is gentle. James wrote, "But the wisdom that comes from heaven is first of all pure; then peace-loving, considerate, submissive, full of mercy and good fruit, impartial and sincere. Peacemakers who sow in peace raise a harvest of righteousness" (3:17-18). The peacemaker is positive. He is tolerant in the best sense of the word. He realizes we are all of fallen stock and so does not demand perfection of others. He is humble. His ego is in hand. And he is loving.

How beautiful true peacemakers are. Filled with peace themselves, they are honest about the state of the relationships around them, whether personal or in the church or in the world. They are honest about what is in their own hearts and sensitive to where others are. They refuse to be satisfied with cheap peace, to say "peace, peace" when there is none. They are willing to risk pain and misunderstanding to make things right. Peacemakers will even *fight* for peace.

The Ultimate Peacemaker

Our Lord Himself is, of course, the supreme peacemaker. He is the glorious "Prince of Peace" prophesied by Isaiah, the messianic fulfillment of the new covenant of peace (cf. Isaiah 9:6; 52:7-10; Ezekiel 37:24-28). At His birth the angels celebrated this fulfillment, singing, "Glory to God in the highest, and on earth peace to men on whom his favor rests" (Luke 2:14).

What we must see is that there was nothing cheap about His

peacemaking. The Apostle Paul wrote, "For God was pleased to have all his fullness dwell in him, and through him to reconcile to himself all things, whether things on earth or things in heaven, by *making peace* through his blood, shed on the cross" (Colossians 1:19-20, italics added). Jesus saw the gravity of our problem, and He refused to sweep it under the rug. Only a drastic solution would suffice, and so He "[made] peace" (the same root words as in Matthew 5:9 for "peacemakers") *"through His blood."* Christ is our supreme example of sacrificial aggression in bringing peace.

He also became the source of peace among all men.

> But now in Christ Jesus you who once were far away have been brought near through the blood of Christ. For he himself is *our peace*, who has made the two one and has destroyed the barrier, the dividing wall of hostility, by abolishing in his flesh the law with its commandments and regulations. His purpose was to create in himself one new man out of the two, thus making peace, and in this one body to reconcile both of them to God through the cross, by which he put to death their hostility. He came and preached peace to you who were far away and peace to those who were near. (Ephesians 2:13-17, italics added)

By His becoming "our peace," He thus dispenses His *shalom* in our hearts. "Peace I leave with you," said Jesus, "my peace I give you" (John 14:27). This, in turn, enables us to promote in each other everything that makes for well-being. The cost of this enabling power is beyond computation. It was attained for us "with the precious blood of Christ, a lamb without blemish or defect" (1 Peter 1:19).

Jesus not only made possible peace with God and peace among men—He gave us the example of how a peacemaker goes about His work.

Do nothing out of selfish ambition or vain conceit, but in humility consider others better than yourselves. Each of you should look not only to your own interests, but also to the interests of others. Your attitude should be the same as that of Christ Jesus: who, being in very nature God, did not consider equality with God something to be grasped, but made himself nothing, taking the very nature of a servant, being made in human likeness. And being found in appearance as a man, he humbled himself and became obedient to death—even death on a cross! (Philippians 2:3-8)

In obtaining our peace, our Lord didn't grasp His glory and dignity, but instead He humbled Himself. The example stands for us who are called to peacemaking. This is expensive! It costs to make peace. Peacemakers are willing to lower themselves, to even lose their dignity in order to bring *shalom* to life. This is the way peacemakers always have been.

A Radical Call

We cannot overemphasize the radical nature of the call to be peacemakers. Peacemaking, as commended by Jesus, is not a natural human quality. It is above human nature. It is impossible. As such, it is a wonder that this Beatitude has been a favorite text of those who know little about Christianity. Secular pacifists love to quote Matthew 5:9 along with Isaiah 2:4 ("They will beat their swords into plowshares and their spears into pruning hooks. Nation will not take up sword against nation, nor will they train for war anymore"). They argue that the Beatitudes (especially the seventh) are "the real gospel"; if only men would practice them, the world would be renewed. Of course, they are correct, as far as they go. For if the Beautiful Attitudes really were practiced, war would be no more. However, peacemaking cannot take place without a radical change in the human heart and the enabling of the Holy Spirit.

The radicalness of Christ's call to peacemaking demands a renovation of human personality. One must first have a profound experience of the *shalom* of God. No one can become a peacemaker until he has found peace himself. The tragedy is that people do not go to the heart of the matter. Without grace, we are natural enemies of God and of one another. Our hearts must be changed. We cannot give what we do not possess.

This inner change, coupled with dependence on the Spirit, is what makes a peacemaker. The Holy Spirit molds the character of peacemakers' lives so that their ethos becomes increasingly gentle, humble, and loving. He elevates their integrity so that they can honestly evaluate the development of peace in their personal lives and society. He steels them *not* to say there is peace when there is no peace. The Spirit leads them to risk pain and misunderstanding in the pursuit of peace. He also leads them in developing the divinely aggressive spirit that wages peace.

Called Sons of God

Now let us consider the sublime benefit: "they will be called sons of God." They have divine paternity, an inheritance from above. The meaning here is breathtaking. Again, as in the six previous Beatitudes, the pronoun is emphatic. The Greek word order is, "for they sons of God shall be called." The idea is that they, and no others, shall be called God's sons. Moreover, the passive voice indicates that it is God, not man, who assigns the title "sons."

The sublimity of this promise comes from the fact that the title "sons of God" refers to character (cf. Luke 6:35). The peacemaker partakes of the character of God. He is like God in the way he lives. No wonder God says, "Blessed are the peacemakers." The proper question to ask next is, what title does God assign to *us*?

Are We Peacemakers?

If we are not peacemakers but troublemakers, there is high probability that we are not true children of God, regardless of how prominently we wear our evangelicalism. Peacemakers are sometimes troublemakers for the sake of peace, but not troublemakers who spread rumors and gossip about others. If you are constantly fomenting discontent, if you find joy in the report of trouble and scandal, if you are omnicritical, always fault-finding, if you are unwilling to be involved in peacemaking, if you are mean—if these negative qualities characterize your life, you are probably not a true Christian (cf. 1 Corinthians 6:9-11; Galatians 5:19-21 on the fate of those involved in slander, hatred, discord, dissension, and factions).

Again, this is not a matter of whether you fall into these things or are struggling to control them, but rather whether these elements are a part of your character. If this is what you are like, then you need to take a day off from your regular schedule and spend it with the Scriptures open before you, seeking the face of God. His Word promises you peace.

> For God was pleased to have all his fullness dwell in him, and through him to reconcile to himself all things, whether things on earth or things in heaven, by making peace through his blood, shed on the cross. (Colossians 1:19-20)

> Therefore, since we have been justified through faith, we have peace with God through our Lord Jesus Christ. . . . For if, when we were God's enemies, we were reconciled to him through the death of his Son, how much more, having been reconciled, shall we be saved through his life! (Romans 5:1, 10)

Now for some advice regarding the "hows" of being a peacemaker. As we first saw, a peacemaker must experience the peace of God himself. The futility of Christians attempting to make peace when their inner lives are walking civil wars is evidenced by the logic that we can impart only that which we possess. If we are believers but have receded from the fullness of Christ's *shalom*, we must come to Him honestly and ask for a fresh implanting of His peace.

Then we must remember that this seventh Beatitude is the last Beatitude that describes the *character* of the Christian, and that all the other Beatitudes build up to it. Peacemakers are developed as they ascend the ladder (the spiritual logic) of the Beatitudes.

Beatitude One: These have experienced poverty of spirit (the recognition that there is nothing within them to commend them to God). In fact, it remains their ongoing awareness and as such is the ground for ongoing spiritual blessing.

Beatitude Two: These have come face to face with their own sin, and they mourn over it.

Beatitude Three: Due to the authenticity of their poverty of spirit and mourning, these experience gentleness and humility in dealing with others.

Beatitude Four: Because these have experienced poverty of spirit and mourning and meekness, they hunger and thirst for all righteousness.

Beatitude Five: The reality of their own need has made these merciful to others.

Beatitude Six: These have been cleansed by the blood of Christ, and their pure lives are focused on Him, and thus they are blessed with an ongoing vision of God.

Beatitude Seven: And now these, having been so infused by Christ's peace and the character of the kingdom, are peacemakers.

Peacemakers are those through whom the entire Beatitudes course again and again—sometimes in order, sometimes out of order, sometimes singly, sometimes all together. They have the character of the King—they are peacemakers.

CHAPTER NINE

THE JOY OF PERSECUTION

"Blessed are those who are persecuted
because of righteousness, for theirs is the
kingdom of heaven."

(MATTHEW 5:10)

From William Blake's *Auguries of Innocence* come these wise, moving lines:

> *Joy and woe are woven fine,*
> *A clothing for the soul divine,*
> *Under every grief and pine*
> *Runs a joy with silken twine.*[1]

Blake understood that joy and woe are part of the fabric of life that God weaves and lovingly fits as perfect clothing for His children. This is mysterious and paradoxical. But there is great comfort in the fact that God is the weaver.

As we take up the final Beatitude we find a divinely composed paradox that has similar mystery, for it involves the relationship of persecution and joy. To read this Beatitude for the first time is shocking. Imagine hearing these lines for the first time ever.

"Blessed are those who are persecuted because of righteousness, for theirs is the kingdom of heaven. Blessed are you when people insult you, persecute you and falsely say all kinds of evil against you because of me. Rejoice and be glad, because great is your reward in heaven, for in the same way they persecuted the prophets who were before you." (Matthew 5:10-12)

One of the Puritan commentators believed that the reason Christ repeated Himself was because the statement was so incredible! And he was probably right.

Until now all the Beatitudes have been given in the third person—"Blessed are those," and that is the way this Beatitude begins. But the repetition in verse 11 changes to the direct address of the second person—"Blessed are *you* when people insult *you*, persecute *you* . . ." The repetition of the Beatitude, its personalization, and its position at the end of the list tell us that it is of supreme importance for the church. Significantly, when stretched on the loom of adversity the church has repeatedly woven persecution and joy into garments of divine praise.

Joy in Prison

Supernatural joy amidst trial has been the experience of the church. When Peter and the other apostles were flogged before the Sanhedrin soon after Pentecost, "the apostles left the Sanhedrin, rejoicing because they had been counted worthy of suffering disgrace for the Name" (Acts 5:41).

Samuel Rutherford, the saintly Scottish pastor, wrote from his prison sty, "I never knew by my nine years of preaching so much of Christ's love, as He taught me in Aberdeen by six months imprisonment." "Christ's cross," he also said, "is such a burden as sails are to a ship or wings to a bird."[2]

And in our own time a Romanian pastor describes how he was imprisoned and tortured mercilessly and yet experienced joy.

Locked in solitary confinement, he had been summoned by his captors, who cut chunks of flesh from his body, and was then returned to his cell, where he was starved. Yet in the midst of this sadism, there were times when the joy of Christ so overcame him that he would pull himself up and shuffle about the cell in holy dance. So remarkable was his joy that on his release from prison and his return to his home, he chose to fast the first day in memorial to the joy he had known in prison.

Hearing stories like these, we naturally ask how it is possible. In partial answer, notice that they did not *enjoy* persecution. To suggest that one should enjoy persecution is to suggest a perversion. We also must understand that persecution of itself is neither blessed nor joyous. However, there is a kind of persecution that has God's blessing and results in joy.

The Persecution That Brings Joy

The Beatitude doesn't say, "Blessed are the persecuted, period!" Unfortunately, this is the way it is sometimes interpreted. And those who read it like this delude themselves into thinking that any time they experience conflict they are bearing the reproach of Christ.

Joseph Bayly's satire *The Gospel Blimp* humorously portrays this fallacy. Some believers in a small town, eager to share their faith, hit on the idea of a gospel blimp. The blimp was piloted back and forth across town, dragging Scripture banners and dropping tracts, called "gospel bombs," into backyards. At first the town's people put up with the intrusion, but their tolerance changed to hostility when the blimp's owners installed a loudspeaker and began assaulting the people with gospel broadcasts. The locals had had enough, and the local newspaper ran an editorial:

> For some weeks now our metropolis has been treated to the spectacle of a blimp with an advertising sign attached at the rear.

> This sign does not plug cigarettes or a bottled beverage, but the religious beliefs of a particular group in our midst. The people of our city are notably broad-minded, and they have good-naturedly submitted to this attempt to proselyte. But last night a new refinement (some would say debasement) was introduced. We refer, of course, to the airborne sound truck, the invader of our privacy, that raucous destroyer of communal peace.[3]

That night the gospel blimp was sabotaged, and of course the Christians saw it as "persecution."

Sadly, Christians are very often persecuted not for their Christianity, but for lack of it. Sometimes they are rejected simply because they have unpleasing personalities. They are rude, insensitive, thoughtless—or piously obnoxious. Some are rejected because they are discerned as proud and judgmental. Others are disliked because they are lazy and irresponsible. Incompetence mixed with piety is sure to bring rejection.

Christ's words must be read in their entirety. "Blessed are those who are persecuted because of righteousness." In context, this is the righteousness (righteous living) taught in the preceding Beatitudes. The world cannot tolerate such a life. Why?

First, poverty of spirit runs counter to the pride of the unbelieving heart. Those whom the world admires are the self-sufficient who need nothing else, not the poor in spirit.

Second, the mourning, repentant heart that sorrows over its own sin and the sins of society is not appreciated by the world.

Third, the gentle and meek person, the one who has the strength not to take up a personal offense, is regarded as weak by those who do not know Christ. Conventional wisdom has it that "meekness is weakness."

Fourth, hungering and thirsting for the spiritual—for Christ—is foreign and repugnant to a world that lusts after only what it can touch and taste.

Fifth, the truly merciful person who not only feels compassion and forgiveness but who gives it is out of step with the grudge-bearing callousness of our age. This person is an awkward, embarrassing rebuke to the uncaring.

Sixth, the pure, single-minded heart focused on God provides a convicting contrast to impure, self-focused culture.

Seventh, the peacemaker is discomforting because he will not settle for a cheap or counterfeit peace and has an embarrassing inclination to wage peace.

The foundational reason such a person will be persecuted is that he or she is like Christ. This is Jesus' point when He completes verse 11 with "because of me" instead of "because of righteousness," used in verse 10. Everyone who lives like Jesus will be persecuted. Listen to Jesus' testimony in John 15:18-20:

> "If the world hates you, keep in mind that it hated me first. If you belonged to the world, it would love you as its own. As it is, you do not belong to the world, but I have chosen you out of the world. That is why the world hates you. Remember the words I spoke to you: 'No servant is greater than his master.' If they persecuted me, they will persecute you also. If they obeyed my teaching, they will obey yours also."

Jesus tells us that since the wind was in His face, it will be in ours too.

Hear Paul's advice to Timothy: "In fact, everyone who wants to live a godly life in Christ Jesus will be persecuted" (2 Timothy 3:12). Paul also warned the Thessalonians, "You know quite well that we were destined for them [trials]. In fact, when we were with you, we kept telling you that we would be persecuted. And it turned out that way, as you well know" (1 Thessalonians 3:3-4). Likewise, he told the Christians in Antioch, "We must go through many hardships to enter the kingdom of God" (Acts 14:22).

Few people who have lived in our time have understood and expressed this better than Dietrich Bonhoeffer:

Suffering, then, is the badge of true discipleship. The disciple is not above his master. . . . That is why Luther reckoned suffering among the marks of the true church, and one of the memoranda drawn up in preparation for the Augsburg Confession similarly defines the church as the community of those "who are persecuted and martyred for the Gospel's sake.". . . Discipleship means allegiance to the suffering Christ, and it is therefore not at all surprising that Christians should be called upon to suffer. In fact, it is a joy and a token of His grace.[4]

During a stressful time in Charles Spurgeon's life when he was depressed by criticism, his wife took a sheet of paper, printed the eight Beatitudes on it in large, old English style script, and tacked it to the ceiling over his bed. She wanted the reality to saturate his mind morning and evening: everyone who lives righteously will be persecuted. There are no exceptions!

How Do We Measure Up?

The logic is revealing: since the first seven Beatitudes describe the character of the true believer, we must conclude that ostracism, persecution, and rejection are just as much signs of the believer as being poor in spirit or merciful. We should not be surprised when persecution comes, but rather, surprised when it does not. Therefore, if the person who claims to follow Christ never experiences any persecution at all, it may be reasonably asked if he really is a Christian.

If we evangelicals have never experienced rejection for the sake of the kingdom, are we citizens of the kingdom? If we have not been out of step with the surrounding culture and suffered its disapproval because we practice the ethics of God's children, are we truly God's children?

Of course, we should be careful not to condemn ourselves if at the moment we are not undergoing persecution. No one is persecuted all the time. Also, we must be careful not to imagine persecution in overly dramatic terms. Most of it is mundane, and some is even quite "civilized."

The Nature of Persecution

The word rendered "persecuted" in Matthew 5:10 bears the root idea of "pursue" or "chase." A good translation is "harass"— "Blessed are the harassed." The reiteration of the Beatitude in verse 11 amplifies this idea: "Blessed are you when men cast insults at you, and persecute you, and say all kinds of evil against you falsely." This casting of insults means literally "to cast in one's teeth," so that the sense here is of throwing insults in one's face. Persecution can go to physical extremes as the church's bloody history records; but most often it is verbal harassment, sometimes audible, sometimes whispered, sometimes direct, sometimes innuendo. Verbal abuse and social ostracism may call for as much heroism as braving the arena.

Other examples of what believers endure include the conscientious worker who has given twenty years of faithful service but has been repeatedly passed over because the brass are uncomfortable with his ethics; or the friendly student who is systematically excluded from conversation because he does not rubber-stamp all that is said; or the housewife who is considered dull by her neighbors because she doesn't delight in their gossip. Such indifference and condescension can sometimes be harder to take than physical violence.

The Real Tragedy of Persecution

These are hard things. But the tragedy today is not that they happen to believers, but that very often, they do not. One reason for this is that many Christians are cut off from the world. They go to a church which is 100 percent Christian, attend Bible studies that are 100 percent Christian, attend Christian schools, exercise with believers, garden with churchgoers, and golf with believers—and thus are sealed from persecution. Others keep their Christianity secret so as not to make waves with non-Christian associates. The tragedy there is that hidden Christianity is probably not Christianity at all.

But by far the greatest reason there is so little persecution is that the church has become like the world. If you want to get along, the formula is simple. Approve of the world's morals and ethics—at least outwardly. Live like the world lives. Laugh at its humor. Immerse yourself in its entertainment. Smile benignly when God is mocked. Act as if all religions converge on the same road. Don't mention hell. Draw no moral judgments. Take no stand on the moral/political issues. Above all, do not share your faith. Follow this formula and it will be smooth sailing.

But the fact is, the church must be persecuted or it is no church at all. People need to be told that if they follow Christ, there will be a price to pay. It will affect how they get along at school. It will affect their profile at the club. It will affect how they make their living.

The early church had no doubt about where a believer's duty lay. One hundred years after Jesus preached the Sermon on the Mount, a man approached the great church father Tertullian with a problem—his business interests and Christianity conflicted. He ended by asking, "What can I do? I must live!" Tertullian replied, "Must you?" When it came to loyalty to Christ and living, Tertullian held that the real Christian chooses Christ.

It is a glorious thing when the church and the individual are persecuted for righteousness' sake, because that means they are like Christ.

The Joy of Persecution

Persecution is glorious because it is the persecuted who know elite joy. In Matthew 5:12 Christ, the ultimate persecuted man, said,

"Rejoice and be glad, because great is your reward in heaven, for in the same way they persecuted the prophets who were before you." The persecuted ought to rejoice in the fact that they keep "classy" company, with the likes of Jeremiah and Elijah.

But the ultimate source of the believer's rejoicing is the ultimate reward, for Jesus says, "great is your reward in heaven." When John D. Rockefeller died, the public became understandably curious about the size of the famous man's fortune. One reporter, determined to find out, secured an appointment with one of Rockefeller's highest aides. He asked the aide how much Rockefeller left behind. The man answered simply, "He left it all."

Not so for those who have been persecuted for the sake of righteousness! The reward is "great," *polus*, which means "immeasurably great." God will not permit what has been done for His glory to go unrewarded. Hear Paul's assurances: "For our light and momentary troubles are achieving for us an eternal glory that far outweighs them all" (2 Corinthians 4:17). "I have fought the good fight, I have finished the race, I have kept the faith. Now there is in store for me the crown of righteousness, which the Lord, the righteous Judge, will award to me on that day—and not only to me, but also to all who have longed for his appearing" (2 Timothy 4:7-8).

What then will it be like for such saints the first thirty seconds in heaven? The first half hour? The first day? The first 10,000 years?

Certainly Christians' persecutions for the sake of righteousness are "as sails to a ship or wings to a bird" in the voyage through life—and on to heaven.

TO BE
BORN AGAIN

F or theirs is the kingdom of heaven" opens and closes the Beatitudes, so that there is no doubt as to the grand theme: the character of those who are in God's kingdom, the heart of authentic believers.

The Beatitudes form a dynamic spiritual logic as seen in the following diagram:

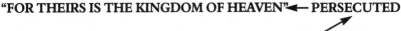

"FOR THEIRS IS THE KINGDOM OF HEAVEN"◄— PERSECUTED

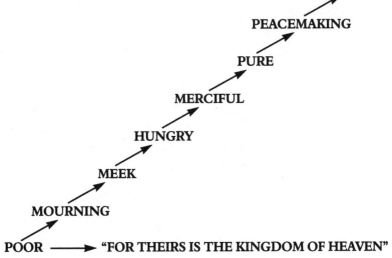

PEACEMAKING

PURE

MERCIFUL

HUNGRY

MEEK

MOURNING

POOR ⟶ "FOR THEIRS IS THE KINGDOM OF HEAVEN"

Of course, no one has perfectly lived all this out, except Jesus. However, as aspects of the character of the kingdom, these are divine indications of whether one truly is part of the kingdom, and also of the health of one's spiritual life.

The Beatitudes undress our inner man. They mirror what is actually within. Dr. Lloyd-Jones explained:

> They really tell us everything about our Christian profession. And if I dislike this kind of thing, if I am impatient with testing, it simply means that my position is entirely contrary to that of the New Testament man. But if I feel, on the other hand, that though these things do search and hurt me, it is good for me to be humbled, and that it is a good thing for me to be held face to face with this mirror, which not only shows me what I am, but what I am in the light of God's pattern for the Christian man, then I have a right to be hopeful about my state and condition.

Perhaps now, having come this far in the book, you have seen yourself as you really are. On the most elementary level, you see yourself as either a Christian or a non-Christian. And hopefully you have been moved by the desire to see your state improved. If an unbeliever, you want to be born again, to be pronounced "blessed," and then to experience the reality of the Beatitudes. If a believer, you want to grow in grace, so that more and more of the character of the kingdom is in you.

If you are not yet a Christian, the following two chapters are for you. The first chapter, entitled "Coming to Christ," provides a profound illustration of what is involved in salvation. The second, entitled "Growing in Christ," gives the unfailing formula for growing in the character of the kingdom.

CHAPTER TEN

COMING TO CHRIST

When he came down from the mountainside,
large crowds followed him. A man with
leprosy came and knelt before him and said,
"Lord, if you are willing, you can make me clean."
Jesus reached out his hand and touched the man.
"I am willing," he said. "Be clean!"
Immediately he was cured of his leprosy.

(MATTHEW 8:1-3)

When Jesus finished giving the Beatitudes, He went on to explain in the remainder of the Sermon on the Mount how a person who had the character of the kingdom lives in the world.

It was the greatest sermon ever preached, and our Lord did not want the teaching to be wasted on His hearers. So He arranged for a living illustration of what is necessary to enter the kingdom. It was an event they would never forget.

A Man in Need of Christ's Touch

This poor man was terribly ill. Dr. Luke, in the parallel account, describes him as "covered with leprosy" (Luke 5:12). So we must understand that the disease had run its course. None of us needs a detailed description of the poor man's loathsome appearance. If you've seen just one picture of someone *covered* with leprosy, it is enough.

What is important to understand is that leprosy, or Hansen's disease as it is better known today (after the man who diagnosed its cause), is not a rotting infection as is commonly thought, nor are its horrible outward physical deformities directly imposed by the disease. In recent years the research of Dr. Paul Brand and others has proven that the disfigurement associated with Hansen's disease comes solely because the body's warning system of pain is destroyed. The disease acts as an anesthetic, bringing numbness to the extremities, as well as to the ears, eyes, and nose. The devastation that follows comes from incidents such as reaching into a charcoal fire to retrieve a dropped potato or washing one's face with scalding water or gripping a tool so tightly that the hands become traumatized and eventually stumplike.[1]

Dr. Brand calls the disease a "painless hell," as well it is. The poor man in our story had not been able to feel for years, and his body, mutilated from head to foot, was foul and rotting.

An Outcast

In Israel the lot of a poor leper was summed up in Leviticus 13:45-46:

> The person with such an infectious disease must wear torn clothes, let his hair be unkempt, cover the lower part of his face and cry out, "Unclean! Unclean!" As long as he has the infection he remains unclean. He must live alone; he must live outside the camp.

We moderns can hardly imagine the humiliation and isolation of a leper's life. He was ostracized from society because it was thought at that time that leprosy was highly contagious (which it is not).

Whenever he came in range of the normal population he had to assume a disheveled appearance and cry, "Unclean! Unclean!" Lepers were typically beggars.

By Jesus' time, rabbinical teaching, with its minute strictures, had made matters even worse. If a leper even stuck his head inside a house, the house was pronounced unclean. It was illegal to greet a leper. Lepers had to remain at least 100 cubits away if they were upwind, and four cubits if downwind. Josephus, the Jewish historian, summed it up by saying that lepers were treated "as if they were, in effect, dead men."[2]

A Representative of Sin

If this were not bad enough, it was also thought that those who had leprosy had contracted the disease because of some great personal sin. People jumped to this erroneous conclusion because in past history such people as Miriam, Uzziah, and Gehazi had been judged with leprosy (cf. Numbers 12:6-10; 2 Chronicles 26:19; and 2 Kings 5:25-27 respectively).

The fact is, the plight of the leper was illustrative of the effects of sin, even though the leper was not any more sinful than anyone else. R. C. Trench, the great Greek scholar and the inspiration for, and first editor of, the monumental *Oxford English Dictionary*, recognized this, saying that though the leper was not worse or guiltier than his fellow Jews, nevertheless he was a parable of sin—an "outward and visible sign of innermost spiritual corruption."[3] The leper is then a physical illustration of ourselves apart from the cleansing work of Christ. For if we could see ourselves with spiritual eyes, apart from Christ, we would be forms of walking death trying to cover ourselves with filthy rags.

Now, looking back to the story, as Christ descends the mountain we must see that His meeting the leper was no chance encounter. The entire meeting was divinely choreographed. We have here not the Sermon on the Mount but the *Sermon on the Move* as He authenticates and illustrates His message. And from the perspective of the leper (*our* perspective), we see what is involved in coming to Christ.

Obtaining the Healing Touch of Christ

The vast throng that had attended Jesus' teaching descended the slope en masse. But suddenly the crowd halted. Matthew exclaims, "A man with leprosy came and knelt before him and said, 'Lord, if you are willing, you can make me clean'" (Matthew 8:2). No doubt the din of the multitude in descent was very considerable. But above it, with increasing clarity, was heard the faint, "Unclean! Unclean!" As if the prow of a boat were moving through the throng, the leper steadily made his way to Jesus as the people fell back, fearing contamination. Perhaps some cursed him, but he kept coming until he was almost to Jesus, crying the refrain of his pitiful life—"Unclean! Unclean!" The Master was face to face with a foul, decaying leper.

Awareness of Sin

In this we see the first and fundamental qualification for coming to Jesus: an awareness of one's condition. The poor man not only said he was unclean—he *knew* he was unclean. If he was prone to any illusions, all he had to do was hold the remainder of his hand up before his eyes and the illusions vanished in an ugly moment. He saw himself as perfectly hopeless. There was nothing he could do to help himself. Everyone else had given up on him too. His many years of illness probably meant that some in his family had even discontinued their prayers for him. In this situation he epitomized the blessed spiritual awareness found in the opening Beatitudes: "Blessed are the poor in spirit, for theirs is the kingdom of heaven.

Blessed are those who mourn, for they will be comforted" (Matthew 5:3-4).

The piteous refrain "Unclean! Unclean!" had shaped the leper's whole psyche. He was a beggar indeed. He truly believed there was nothing within him commendable to God. He was in the perfect posture to receive grace.

God does not come to the self-sufficient, those who think they have no need or imagine that they can make it on their own. He comes to the bankrupt in spirit, those who mourn their condition. It is very probable that the leper had been sitting beyond the range of the crowd, transfixed by Jesus' opening words and the masterful argument that followed, and that the Holy Spirit so overwhelmed him that nothing could keep him from Jesus.

If you would come to Christ, this is the way you must come—saying, "Unclean! Unclean!" In fact, if you come saying, "Only partly unclean" or "25 percent clean" or "10 percent clean," He will not receive you. Have you come to Christ like the leper? It is the only way He receives us and gives us the healing touch. This is the first qualification for meeting Christ.

Worshipful Submission

The next qualification is in the first sentence of Matthew 8:2: "A man with leprosy came and *knelt before him*" (italics added). This is worshipful submission. The word used to describe his bowing takes us into the leper's heart. The basic meaning of the word in early Greek literature was "to kiss," as in kissing the earth as one lay prostrate to the gods. In the Old Testament (Septuagint) it was used to translate the Hebrew word for *bowing down*.[4] Luke tells us he "fell with his face to the ground" (Luke 5:12), which enhances the picture. The humble leper put his whole soul into adoration as he lay prostrate before Christ. He submitted to Christ as the only possible source of his healing. The lesson is clear for us. Christ's healing touch doesn't come with a casual, irreverent acknowledgment. It comes as we bow before Him in realization that He is our *only* hope.

Real Faith

The third factor in obtaining the healing touch of Christ is faith. The whole of Matthew 8:2 reads, "A man with leprosy came and knelt before him and said, 'Lord, if you are willing, you can make me clean.'" Mark indicates that he repeated this several times (1:40). How poignant the picture is with the leper, still prostrate, repeating in the hoarse voice typical of those with advanced leprosy, "Lord, if you are willing, you can make me clean—Lord, if you are willing, you can make me clean." No doubt he had heard of Jesus' miraculous power, had been listening to Him that day, and had come to the conclusion that Christ was omnipotent. Christ had the power. But what is more significant is that the leper said, "You can make *me* clean." He believed that Jesus could save even *him*. We must all believe this if we are to receive grace.

How do we obtain His healing touch? We recognize our sinful condition; we bow before Him in reverence as the only source of our healing; and we believe that He can do it for *us*.

Experiencing the Healing Touch of Christ

As the leper lay at Jesus' feet, Jesus looked on him as he had never before been viewed. According to Mark's Gospel, Christ was "filled with compassion" (1:41), indicating that Jesus was so touched by what He saw that He had a visceral reaction.

Then came the height of the encounter: "Jesus reached out his hand and touched the man" (Matthew 8:3). Perhaps it had been twenty or even thirty years since the leper had been touched by a non-leprous hand. Perhaps he was a father and had once known the embrace of his children and his wife, but for years he had not known even a touch. Now he received the touch of Christ—and as Bishop Westcott says, the word "expresses more than superficial contact."[5] It is often translated "to take hold of." Jesus, at the very least, placed His hand firmly on the leper.

How beautiful Christ is. He didn't have to do that. He could have spoken a word or simply willed the healing. But He chose to lay His hand on the poor man in front of the multitude. The onlookers were appalled. The disciples were shocked. Jesus was now ceremonially unclean—and besides He might catch the disease, they thought. Why did Jesus do it? There are some very human reasons. Reaching out was the reflex of His life. It was the instinct of His loving heart. But He also wanted to clear away any fears the man had. He wanted the leper to *feel* His willingness and sympathy. The touch said, "I'm with you. I understand."

Those were the human reasons, but there was an overshadowing theological reason. The touch of His pure hand on the rotting leper is a parable of the Incarnation. Jesus in the Incarnation laid hold of our flesh. He took on flesh, became sin for us, and thus gave us His purity. "God made him who had no sin to be sin for us, so that in him we might become the righteousness of God" (2 Corinthians 5:21). Jesus lays hold of our flesh. He touches us and heals us.

The Miracle

Matthew concludes: "Jesus reached out his hand and touched the man. 'I am willing,' he said. 'Be clean!' Immediately he was cured of his leprosy" (8:3). The cleansing was instantaneous. The healing was *sudden* and *complete*. His feet—toeless, ulcerated stubs—were suddenly whole, bursting his shrunken sandals. The knobs on his hands grew fingers before his very eyes. Back came his hair, eyebrows, eyelashes. Under his hair were ears, and before him a nose. His skin was supple and soft. Can you hear a thundering roar from the multitude? Can you hear the man crying *not* "Unclean! Unclean!" but rather, "I'm clean! I'm clean!"

That is what Jesus Christ can do for you in an instant, in a split second of belief.

The lessons of the leper are three. If you would be healed you must:

- Come to Christ with a deep awareness of your sin. Do you now acknowledge that you are a sinner and that you have nothing in yourself to commend you to God? Do you mourn your sin? If so, you are ready.
- Bow before Him in humble reverence. Submit to Him as your only hope. Tell God that if He does not save you, you will be lost.
- Believe that He can do it. Say, "Lord, if You are willing, You can make me clean." Believe this word: "He himself bore our sins in his body on the tree, so that we might die to sins and live for righteousness; by his wounds you have been healed" (1 Peter 2:24). Do you truly believe this verse of Scripture? Then put your name in it: "He himself bore _____'s sins on the tree, so that _____ might die to sins and live for right-eousness; by his wounds _____ has been healed." If you believe it, thank Him! You have been born again!

If you have not done this, do not read another page until the matter is settled. Right now nothing else matters. Do it now.

CHAPTER ELEVEN

GROWING IN CHRIST

"Ask and it will be given to you;
seek and you will find;
knock and the door will be opened to you."

(MATTHEW 7:7)

When Howard Carter, the British archaeologist, first peered wide-eyed into the ancient Egyptian tomb he had just opened, he saw nothing. The year was 1922. For more than twenty centuries archaeologists, tourists, and tomb robbers had searched for the burial places of Egypt's pharaohs. It was believed that nothing remained undisturbed, especially in the Royal Valley where the ancient monarchs had been buried for millennia. With only a few scraps of evidence, Carter carried on his pursuit, personally financed because no one felt there was anything left to be discovered. Somewhere . . . somehow . . . he was convinced that one tomb remained. Twice during his six-year search he was within two yards of the first stone step leading to the burial chamber.

"Can you see anything?" his assistants asked as Howard Carter's eyes adjusted to the semidarkness. Carter *was* seeing! But he had difficulty speaking because he was looking at what no modern man had ever seen. Wooden animals, statues, chests, chariots, carved cobras, vases, daggers, jewels, a throne . . . and a hand-carved coffin of a teenage king. It was, of course, the priceless tomb and treasure of King Tutankhamen, the world's most exciting archaeological discovery.

Howard Carter's perseverance is to be applauded, for because of his steadfastness he succeeded where others had failed. In the spiritual realm such doggedness is even more commendable, because it too will bring success where others have failed. Those who learn to ask, seek, and knock will find. And the treasure will far exceed that of King Tut.

Spiritual Treasure

Jesus' words recorded in Matthew 7:7-11 describe the way a man or woman who understands what the Sermon on the Mount is all about will pray. The instruction that Jesus gives on prayer should not be lifted from its context in the Sermon and abused, as is so common today. All of us have heard it done. It goes something like this: "The Bible says, 'Ask and it will be given to you; seek and you will find; knock and the door will be opened to you.' Therefore, all we have to do is ask for it with faith and persistence, and we will get it. 'You do not have, because you do not ask God' (James 4:2)—so go for it! Name it and claim it!" This view sees God as a celestial slot machine. Pull the handle enough times in prayer and you will surely get what you want.

Such thinking is entirely wrong. A text apart from its context is a pretext. So we must refrain from isolating "ask . . . seek . . . knock" from its context, for the context is eminently spiritual. The broad context of the Sermon sets down the surpassing righteousness, humility, sincerity, purity, and love expected of those who are members of the kingdom of God. These virtues are beyond human attainment apart from God's grace. The broad context underscores our spiritual need.

Likewise, the context immediately before "ask . . . seek . . . knock" is explicitly spiritual. In Matthew 7:1-6 Jesus has shown us the danger of condemning other people as if we were judges. He also has told us to remove the log from our own eye before attempting to remove the speck from someone else's. His warning is, "For in the same way you judge others, you will be judged, and with the measure you use, it will be measured to you" (v. 2). This standard is terrifying. How can we live up to it? The answer is: we need to be cleansed. We need God's help and His grace. But from where? And Jesus answers, "Ask and it will be given to you; seek and you will find; knock and the door will be opened to you" (v. 7).

This famous text is not one to apply to our material desires. *It tells us how to pray for the character of the kingdom in our lives.*

Persistence

Jesus begins with some advice about attitude:

> "Ask and it will be given to you; seek and you will find; knock and the door will be opened to you. For everyone who asks receives; he who seeks finds; and to him who knocks, the door will be opened." (Matthew 7:7-8)

The Lord's language is unusually compelling because the three verbs "ask," "seek," and "knock" indicate an ascending intensity.

- "Ask" implies requesting assistance for a conscious need. We realize our lack and thus ask for help. The word also suggests humility in asking, for it is commonly used of one asking a superior.
- "Seek" involves asking but adds action. The idea is not just to express our need, but to get up and look around for help. It involves effort.

119

- "Knock" includes asking plus acting plus persevering—like someone who keeps pounding on a closed door.

The stacking of these words is extremely forceful, and the fact that they are present imperatives gives them even more punch. The text actually reads: "*Keep on asking*, and it shall be given to you; *keep on seeking*, and you shall find; *keep on knocking*, and it shall be opened to you." This picture is of a man who will not stop knocking.

Intense Asking

These verses are remarkably intense—and there is no doubt that our Lord meant for them to be understood in this way. In one of His prayer parables in the Gospel of Luke, the Lord urges the same intensity:

> Then Jesus told his disciples a parable to show them that they should always pray and not give up. He said: "In a certain town there was a judge who neither feared God nor cared about men. And there was a widow in that town who kept coming to him with the plea, 'Grant me justice against my adversary.' For some time he refused. But finally he said to himself, 'Even though I don't fear God or care about men, yet because this widow keeps bothering me, I will see that she gets justice, so that she won't eventually wear me out with her coming!'" And the Lord said, "Listen to what the unjust judge says." (Luke 18:1-6)

The cultivation of persistence in one's prayer life was evidently a recurring motif in Jesus' teaching on prayer. And here in Matthew 7:7, which is subject to the immense spiritual force of what has been said in the Sermon on the Mount, Christ's point is this: *we are to passionately persist in prayer for the elements of spiritual growth*. We naturally persevere in our prayers when one close to us is ill. Likewise, if we are in financial trouble, or if we are expecting a promotion, or if we have some frightening task ahead of us, we pray intensely.

But the question is: do we persist in our prayers for spiritual growth for ourselves and others? Do we "ask . . . seek . . . knock" for poverty of spirit? Do we keep knocking for a merciful attitude, or for a pure heart, or to be peacemakers? On the whole, most Christians do not. And the reason is they have never understood that in this text Christ is encouraging the pursuit of spiritual things rather than material. Consider what would happen to Christianity if God's people understood what Christ is saying here and put it to work. We will return to this thought later.

Intense Need

Apart from correctly understanding this verse, only a sensed need for God's grace will drive us to passionate prayer for our spiritual development. First, we see what the kingdom requires as to righteousness. It is perfection (Matthew 5:48). We are to be holy as He is holy (Leviticus 19:2). Only the pure in heart will see God (Matthew 5:8). Then we see ourselves, and we know that though we do good things, we are evil; that all of us, Jews and Greeks, are under sin (Romans 3:9). The dual sight of His perfect standard and our own sin drives us to our knees and to His grace. We learn that there is no hope for spiritual improvement apart from grace. Only the one who sees this reality rejoices to read Jesus' invitation to ask, seek, and knock.

Let Jesus' words rest heavily upon us. We are to ask and keep on asking for those things that will make us more like Him. We are to seek and keep on seeking. We are to knock and keep on knocking. Perseverance is the key to God's treasure, as it has often proved to be in the matters of earthly treasure, as with Howard Carter.

But how much greater our rewards when we persevere in

praying for God's treasures. Exaggeration? We think not. King Tut's treasure brought him no happiness; and if we were as rich as he, the effect would be the same. Besides, King Tut left it all behind. But the treasure Christ gives is eternally ours and eternally satisfying.

We may wonder why God wants us to persist intensely for things He surely wants to give us. The answer lies with us. He wants to give us all things, but He cannot give them until we are ready. Persistent prayer for them prepares us.

Confidence

The last part of Jesus' command teaches us that we are not only to pray with persistence but with confidence. The verses we have studied shout assurance to us: "Ask and it will be given to you; seek and you will find; knock and the door will be opened to you." The only condition for our receiving spiritual treasure is persistence. If we persistently ask, we *will* receive it.

I am grateful this verse is not a blank check for anything in life. I am thankful it cannot be applied to literally anything we want. Dr. Howard Hendricks recalls that when he was a young man certain mothers had set their hopes on him in behalf of their daughters. One mother even said to him, "Howard, I just want you to know I am praying that you will be my son-in-law." Says Dr. Hendricks of this, "Have you ever thanked God for unanswered prayer?" I am grateful that God has not answered all my prayers too. And so are you. On the other hand, how wonderful it is that He has always answered our persistent prayers for spiritual growth.

The Father Answers Our Prayers

Jesus assures us that this is true with an illustration based on earthly fatherhood: "Which of you, if his son asks for bread, will give him a stone? Or if he asks for a fish, will give him a snake?" (Matthew 7:9-10).

The illustration is absurd. The Galileans who first heard it were familiar with the flat stones on the seashore that looked exactly like their round, flat cakes of bread; they were also aware that fish (more likely eels) looked very much like snakes. The picture is of a son coming to ask his father for something to eat and his father replying, "Here, son, enjoy!" as the boy cracks his teeth. "Oh, you did not like that? Here, have a fish," and he gives him a harmful snake or eel. No true father would be so ignorant or cruel. Fathers give what is good.

The Lord crowns His assurance with the example of the Heavenly Father's giving: "If you, then, though you are evil, know how to give good gifts to your children, how much more will your Father in heaven give good gifts to those who ask him!" (v. 11). This is the familiar *a fortiori* argument that Jesus is so fond of. If it is true of the lesser, how much more of the greater. God is our Father, our *Abba*, our dearest Father *par excellence*! Think of our earthly fathers at their very best and multiply their best by heaven and we have it. Isaiah says of the Father's care, "Can a mother forget the baby at her breast and have no compassion on the child she has borne? Though she may forget, I will not forget you!" (49:15). The "how much more" of our text has an infinite ring to it.

The Holy Spirit Answers Our Prayers

An earthly father would never give his child a stone for bread, but sometimes he makes mistakes. Earthly fathers may think they are doing the right thing only to discover it is absolutely wrong. God never errs, though in fact it *is* His policy to give greater quality and quantity than we imagine in our prayers.

Luke's parallel quotation gives us a remarkable insight into the mechanics of God's giving more of "what is good" to those who ask Him: "If you then, though you are evil, know how to give good gifts to your children, how much more will your Father in heaven give the Holy Spirit to those who ask him!" (Luke 11:13). Luke's sub-stitution of "Holy Spirit" for "what is good" is no contradiction because it is the Holy Spirit who bestows what is good. Moreover, the Holy Spirit knows what we need better than we do! The Apostle Paul informs us:

> In the same way, the Spirit helps us in our weakness. We do not know what we ought to pray for, but the Spirit himself inter-cedes for us with groans that words cannot express. And he who searches our hearts knows the mind of the Spirit, because the Spirit intercedes for the saints in accordance with God's will. (Romans 8:26-27)

The result is, we get more of "what is good" than we ever imagined.

Our assurance is this: if we ask for anything (*anything!*) that is good for us spiritually, God will give it to us. If you do not have eter-nal life through Jesus Christ, you may be sure that He will give it to you if you truly ask. If you are a believer but are short on Christian graces, you must ask, and you will receive. If you are untruthful but are willing to ask, seek, and knock for truthfulness, He will give you the spirit of truth. If you are ungenerous and will bring this attitude to God in passionate prayer, He will give you a generous spirit. If you are unkind but will passionately seek God for a kind heart, He will give it to you.

We Must Pray

Now think what would happen if we prayed for our spiritual growth as intensely as we pray for our physical needs. The church would explode, because a far greater proportion of its people would be living kingdom lives. Our pulpits would be filled with preach-ers of power. The mission fields would shrink as thousands more would pour out to the harvest—with greater power.

Pray Persistently

Do we want the character of the kingdom in our lives? Then we have to do two things. First, we must ask persistently. Jesus says we are to "ask and keep on asking; seek and keep on seeking; knock and keep on knocking." We are to beseech God constantly and passionately for spiritual blessing.

Pray Confidently

We are at the same time to ask confidently. Everyone who asks this way receives; and everyone who seeks like this finds; and everyone who knocks and keeps on knocking has a door opened to him or her. God will give us anything we ask for that is good for us spiritually. If we do not have, it is our fault, for as James says, "You do not have, because you do not ask God" (James 4:2). Over 200 years ago John Newton wrote about this very thing in one of his great hymns:

> *Come, my soul, thy case prepare;*
> *Jesus loves to answer prayer;*
> *He Himself has bid thee pray,*
> *Therefore will not say thee nay.*
>
> *Thou art coming to a King;*
> *Large petitions with thee bring;*
> *For His grace and power are such,*
> *None can ever ask too much.*

We can never ask too much spiritually. Let us ask and receive.

Someone once said, "Any discussion of the doctrine of prayer that does not issue in the practice of prayer is not only *not* helpful but harmful." That is true. If God is speaking to you, you must pray.

- First, single out the spiritual qualities that you would like to cultivate. In reference to the Beatitudes, it may be poverty of spirit or meekness or purity of heart. Write them on your prayer list, and begin to regularly pray.
- Second, as you pray, pray persistently—asking, seeking, knocking. Seek with all your being.
- Third, know this: that you *will* receive them. And they will be better than you have dreamed, because your Heavenly Father will give them to you. You will be blessed because His smile will be upon you.

TO BE A BLESSING

What happens when the character of the kingdom is not only rooted but flourishes in our lives? The Lord Jesus answers this question by framing the Beatitudes with two brilliant metaphors.

First, *salt*: "You are the salt of the earth. But if the salt loses its saltiness, how can it be made salty again? It is no longer good for anything, except to be thrown out and trampled by men" (Matthew 5:13).

Second, *light*: "You are the light of the world. A city on a hill cannot be hidden. Neither do people light a lamp and put it under a bowl. Instead they put it on its stand, and it gives light to everyone in the house. In the same way, let your light shine before men, that they may see your good deeds and praise your Father in heaven" (Matthew 5:14-16).

Lord, make the Beatitudes grow in us, so that we may be salt to a decaying world and light in the midst of darkness. Amen.

CHAPTER TWELVE

BE SALT!

"You are the salt of the earth. But if the
salt loses its saltiness, how can it be made
salty again? It is no longer good for
anything, except to be thrown out
and trampled by men."

(MATTHEW 5:13)

Realizing that the Beatitudes are essentially interior, one might be tempted to think that they can be lived in isolation, away from the contradictory world. But it is just the opposite. It is impossible to live these eight characteristics of the kingdom in private. They are powerfully social when put to work. And that is why Christ crowns them with two brilliant and searching metaphors (salt and light), which tell us how those who live the Beatitudes must relate to the world.

The Salted Church

Knowing the situation as we do, that Christ had only a few poor, uneducated followers, His words no doubt appeared to some as presumptuous and even absurd. "You, you alone, are the salt of the earth—not just in Palestine, but throughout the whole earth." The Lord was saying that His followers would perform a universal task that would affect all mankind. He was expressing a mysterious confidence that would be borne out by history.

The Salted Church, a Preservative

What did Jesus mean by, "You are the salt of the earth"? Fundamental to understanding His statement is the fact that in the ancient world the primary function of salt was as a preservative. There were no ice-making machines in the first century. Refrigeration was beyond man's wildest dreams. The only way to preserve meat was to salt it down or soak it in a saline solution. In fact, this was common practice right into the twentieth century in remote areas of the world. It was particularly the experience of pioneer missionaries. As one describes it:

> This was absolutely imperative. Under the high temperatures and hot weather of the region, decay and decomposition of meat was astonishingly rapid. We had no winter weather, or cool, frosty nights to chill the flesh. Besides this, swarms of ubiquitous flies soon hovered over the butchered carcasses. The only way to prevent them from ruining the meat . . . was to soak the slabs of meat in a strong solution of salt.[1]

As a matter of historical interest, this preserving quality of salt was what made it possible for David Livingstone's body to be shipped back to England for interment in Westminster Abbey. Having died in deepest Africa, Livingstone's servant buried the great missionary's heart in African soil and then salted his body and shipped it home for an honored burial. Salt is a powerful preservative indeed!

The logical implication of "You are the salt of the earth" is that the world tends toward rot and decomposition. Jesus was under no illusion about the world apart from Himself. When the world is left to itself, it tends to fester and putrefy, for the germs of evil are everywhere present and active. This is the consistent teaching of Scripture and of biblical history. The world was a perfect creation, but sin came and decay set in, with the result that it became so rotten that God removed virtually the entire population by the Flood. Given another chance, there was immediate debauchery—and with time came the destruction of Sodom and Gomorrah. We live in a world that constantly tends toward decay. Christless structures may look okay on the outside, but inside they are rotting away.

Jesus says in effect: "Humanity without Me is a dead body that is rotting and falling apart. And, you, My followers, are the salt that must be rubbed into the flesh to halt the decomposition." Indeed, the church must be rubbed into the world—into its rotting flesh and wounds—so that it might be preserved.

This matter of being salt has positive and negative aspects. On the negative side, the presence of a salty Christian will retard decay, simply because his or her life is a reproach to the sin of those around him or her. There are certain people whose presence invites a filthy story, while there are others around whom no one would think of being coarse. It is not because the salty Christian is self-righteous or condemning, but rather because his life is of such a quality that evil conversation seems shabby and inappropriate. This is due to the presence of Christ in that person.

Such Christians exert a precious influence on society. Their lives reduce crime, restrain ethical corruption, promote honesty, quicken the conscience, and elevate the general moral atmosphere. The presence of such people in the military, in business, in education, or in a fraternity or sorority will amazingly elevate the level of living. And their absence will hasten surprising depths of depravity. Believers, salty believers, are the world's preservative. The question we must ask ourselves is, what happens when we get to know people who do not know Christ? Does our presence make a difference for them? Are we salt?

The Salted Church, a Spice

There is also the positive aspect. Not only are Christians' lives meant to reprove evil—they are also meant to elicit the best from those around them, though, sad to say, not everyone who claims to be a Christian has this effect. Playwright Henrik Ibsen put this complaint on the lips of the Roman Emperor Julian:

> Have you looked at these Christians closely? Holloweyed, pale-cheeked, flat-breasted all; they brood their lives away, unspurted by ambition: the sun shines for them, but they do not see it: the earth offers them its fullness, but they desire it not; all their desire is to renounce and to suffer that they may come to die.[2]

Similarly, Keats portrayed Julian's complaint, "Thou hast conquered, O pale Galilean."

The truth is, that is the way life is without Christ. Life apart from Christ is insipid and dull. That is why our culture attempts to numb itself with pleasure and drugs. People are literally dying of boredom. The entertainment industry does its best to make life look otherwise. Fictional good is made out to be boring and flat, while fictional evil is portrayed as exciting and intriguing; but it is actually the other way around. As Simone Weil said, "Nothing is so beautiful, nothing so continually fresh and surprising, so full of sweet and perpetual ecstasy, as the good: no desert is so dreary, monotonous, and boring as evil."[3]

In biblical times, as today, salt was not only a preservative but a condiment. Christianity is what brings spice and zest to life. The bland is made savory; the unpalatable becomes a delight.

Believers must be salty not only because they are righteous, but because they have life indeed! They ought to write the best books, be the most courteous, work the hardest, be the best musicians and artists, craftsmen and students.

The Salted Church, a Thirst Stimulator

Jesus made people thirsty for God the Father. Whenever anyone encountered Jesus, whether a Pharisee like Nicodemus or an outcast like Mary Magdalene, that person became spiritually thirsty. Are we salty enough to make people thirsty for Jesus?

At dinner one bite is enough to know whether the food has been salted or not. Just a pinch of salt goes a long way. William Wilberforce, the man who almost singlehandedly brought about the anti-slavery Emancipation Bill in England, is living proof of this. Dwarfed by disease, he did not appear to be much of a force for anything. However, James Boswell wrote of him, after listening to one of his speeches, "I saw a shrimp mount the table; but as I listened, he grew and grew until the shrimp became a whale."[4] Tiny, elfish, misshapen, he was salt to British society, not only bringing preservation but enticement to Christ by his beautiful life. Even a little salt will make its presence felt.

The Desalted Church

Our Lord acknowledges the tragedy of a desalted church with the words, "if the salt has become tasteless"(NASB). Chemically, salt is an extremely stable compound and does not become tasteless. The consensus of scholars is that Jesus was referring to its adulteration or dilution. It is dangerously easy for Christians to become diluted and to lose their preserving influence in the world. We cannot look at Christianity at large or at American Christianity or at local Christianity or at our own hearts without admitting that the possibility of saltless, insipid, bland Christianity is very real.

If we are not affecting the world, the world is affecting us. We are to export our influence to those around us, but if there are more imports than exports—if there are greater influences coming in than going out—we will become like the world. If we are not salting the world, the world is rotting us.

We must ask ourselves if there is any difference between our approach to materialism and that of the world. Are there any distinctions between our approach to pleasure and that of unbelievers? Do we approach happiness differently? Is there a difference in our ethics?

The Resalted Church

What is the hope for a desalted church? The Lord raises this question by asking, "How will it [salt] be made salty again?"(NASB). As we have seen, salt cannot lose its saltiness, and so here we must affirm that it cannot be made salty. In His ancient context, Christ is saying that if salt has lost its savor (has been diluted), there is no *natural* hope for it. Is there any natural hope for us if we have lost our savor by worldly dilution? The answer is no. However, Jesus extends the metaphor into the supernatural, and here we must answer yes! Jesus is not teaching that if a Christian loses his pungency, he cannot get it back. Nothing but our own sin can keep us from becoming salty.

An acquaintance in his sixties was resalted. His Christian life had become compromised and useless. But God graciously confronted him with his condition, and he committed his life to Christ. During the last ten years of his life he has had an incredibly salty effect on the world. His life, in fact, has touched thousands!

There is urgency in Jesus' words, and it is found in the concluding sentence of Matthew 5:13 where He warns of the destiny of saltless salt: "It is no longer good for anything, except to be thrown out and trampled by men." Since it is useless, it will be tossed onto the road where perhaps it will fill in a few cracks and be further dissipated. There it will sterilize the soil, retard plant growth, and make the surroundings barren. This substance, so beneficial to life in its pungent, pure form, brings desolation when cast aside. What a sad description of the Christian life that has lost its saltiness.

Such is the testimony of church history. We search in vain for the once-great church of Asia Minor with its flourishing parishes. The church of North Africa where the great Augustine ministered is nonexistent. Salt that lost its saltiness was cast out and trodden under foot by the men of the world.

Be Salt

Yet despite the church's failures, Christ's use of this metaphor is boldly positive. Jesus says, "You (you alone) are the salt of the earth." Jesus believes in us. He is optimistic. Jesus believes that we can have a healing, preserving influence on our own society and the world. He believes that we can bring flavor to life—that we can make the world thirsty for Him. And the church has done just that again and again.

We are salt! Christ wants us to cultivate our saltiness by constantly communing with Him and being constantly filled with the Spirit. He wants us to get out of the salt shaker and into the world—rubbing ourselves into its rotting wounds.

He wants us to remember that though we are not much, a little salt goes a long way!

CHAPTER THIRTEEN

BE LIGHT!

"You are the light of the world. A city on a hill
cannot be hidden. Neither do people light a lamp and
put it under a bowl. Instead they put it on its stand,
and it gives light to everyone in the house.
In the same way, let your light shine before men,
that they may see your good deeds and praise
your Father in heaven."

(MATTHEW 5:14-16)

The Illumination of the Temple, a spectacular night-time cere-
mony, took place in the temple treasury before four massive
golden candelabra topped with huge torches. It is said that the candelabra were as tall as the highest walls of the temple, and that at the
top of these candelabra were mounted great bowls that held sixty-
five liters of oil. There was a ladder for each candelabrum, and
when evening fell, healthy young priests would carry oil up to the
great bowls and light the protruding wicks. Eyewitnesses said that
the huge flames that leapt from these torches illuminated not only
the temple but all of Jerusalem. *The Mishna* tells us:

> Men of piety and good works used to dance before them [the candelabra] with burning torches in their hands singing songs and praises and countless Levites played on harps, lyres, cymbals, and trumpets and instruments of music.[1]

This exotic rite celebrated the great pillar of fire (the glorious cloud of God's presence) that led the Israelites during their sojourn in the wilderness and spread its fiery billows over the tabernacle.

It was in the temple treasury the following morning, with the charred torches still in place, that Jesus lifted His voice above the crowd and proclaimed, "I am the light of the world." There could scarcely be a more emphatic way to announce one of the supreme truths of His existence. Christ was saying, "The pillar of fire that came between you and the Egyptians, the cloud that guided you by day in the wilderness and illumined the night and enveloped the tabernacle, the glorious cloud that filled Solomon's temple, was Me!" He announced, "I am the light of the world. Whoever follows me will never walk in darkness, but will have the light of life" (John 8:12).

Jesus is the light of the world! He is everything suggested by the storied cloud of glory. And He is everything suggested by the sublime metaphor of light—and much more!

The immense truth that Christ is the light of the world must control our thinking as we now take up the unforgettable words of Matthew 5:14-16, where He applies the metaphor to *us*.

The World Is in Darkness

The truth that Jesus is the light of the world is indeed a glorious one, but it suggests the equally but inglorious truth that the world is in darkness. A spiritual darkness dominates the entire world system, and it is terrible.

But the deeper horror is that the inhabitants of the earth love it. John wrote, "This is the verdict: Light has come into the world, but men loved darkness instead of light because their deeds were evil" (John 3:19). Darkness by itself is one thing, but intentional darkness is far worse. To be subject to the darkness of the night before the dawn is one thing, but it is quite another thing to deliberately live down in the earth among the caves and the bats, refusing to come to the light.

Why this preference? John tells us that the world loves darkness because its deeds are evil. Unconsciously, and sometimes consciously, the world reasons very much like Lady Macbeth:

> Com', thick night, and pall thee in the dunnest smoke of hell,
> that my keen knife see not the wound it makes, nor heaven peep
> through the blanket of the dark.[2]

It is a grim picture, but it is biblical and therefore true: the world is in darkness.

We Are Light

It is the reality of the world's darkness that makes Jesus' pronouncement so thrilling: "You (you alone) are the light of the world." If we are truly believers, we are the light of the world. To say such a thing about ourselves without divine precedent and sanction would be the height of arrogance. But Christ says it, and it is easily one of the most amazing statements to ever fall from His lips—especially realizing what we are like. It is a fact: *we are light!*

How can this possibly be? Dr. Donald Grey Barnhouse explained it this way: when Christ was in the world, He was like the shining sun that is here in the day and gone at night. When the sun sets, the moon comes up; and the moon is a picture of the believers, or the church. The church shines, but it does not shine with its own light. It shines with *reflected* light. When Jesus was in the world He said, "I am the light of the world." But as He contemplated leaving the world, He told His disciples, "You are the light of the world." At times the church has been a full moon dazzling the world with an almost daytime light. These have been times of great enlightenment, such as those of Paul and Luther and Wesley. And at other times the church has been only a thumbnail moon—and very little light shines on the earth. But whether the church is a full moon or a new thumbnail moon, waxing or waning, it reflects the light of the sun.³

How Mysterious

However, the Scriptures teach that our light is more than reflected; we, in fact, *become* light ourselves. The Apostle Paul said, "For you were once darkness, but now you are light in the Lord. Live as children of light" (Ephesians 5:8). Somehow our incorporation in Christ allows us to some extent to *be* light. Our light is still derived from Him—not a ray of it comes from ourselves; but it is more than reflected. We have been made to "participate in the divine nature," as Peter says (2 Peter 1:4). This is a mystery.

But the beautiful thing, mystery that it is, is that it works! The church has had some great lights. When the English martyrs Hugh Latimer and Nicholas Ridley were being taken to the stake for burning, Latimer turned to Ridley and said, "Be of good cheer, Brother Ridley, we have lighted such a candle in England as by the grace of God shall never be put out." Latimer and Ridley continue to burn as shining lights in the world.

There are also lesser lights, for the mystery works for all believers, even children. When my now-grown daughter Holly was in kindergarten, she weekly approached her teacher, Mrs. Smith, and timidly said, "Mrs. Smith, will you come to church?" Mrs. Smith would promise to attend. And when Mrs. Smith didn't show, Holly would again approach Mrs. Smith on Monday morning and say, "Mrs. Smith, you didn't come to church." Who could resist those big, sad, brown eyes? Finally Mrs. Smith came, and she came again, and she came to know Jesus. And today she is a remark-able, radiant sunbeam herself. This is a mystery, and it is beautiful. The facts are: first, Jesus is the light; second, the world is in dark-ness; and third, somehow believers are light. Believers shine.

How to Shine

Seeing that we are light, how can we shine more? Consider this: a man returning from a journey brought his wife a matchbox that would glow in the dark. After giving it to her she turned out the light, but the matchbox could not be seen. Both thought they had been cheated. Then the wife noticed some French words on the box and called a friend to translate. And this is what the inscription said:

> *If you want me to shine in the night,*
> *keep me in the light.*

So it is with us! We must expose ourselves to Jesus, revel in His Word, and spend time in prayer soaking up His rays. As Paul wrote, "And we, who with unveiled faces all reflect the Lord's glory, are being transformed into his likeness with ever-increasing glory, which comes from the Lord, who is the Spirit" (2 Corinthians 3:18).

The Ministry of Light

Turning us from the spiritual *facts* of light to its *function* in this world, Jesus presents two scenes.

As Cities on Hills

First, Jesus says, "A city on a hill cannot be hidden" (Matthew 5:14). There is no way to obscure a city on the crest of a hill. Quito, Ecuador, situated at 10,000 feet, illumines the sky for 75 miles around. It cannot be hidden. Yet when one is in the great city itself, the lights from the tiny villages even higher above in the Andes are easily seen as well.

Believers are like this. They characteristically are visible. As Martyn Lloyd-Jones said, "If we find in ourselves a tendency to put the light under a bushel, we must begin to examine ourselves and make sure that it really is light."[4] This is wise, gracious advice! Do we hide our light? If so, are we really light?

Christians are visible, and this visibility makes them like the beckoning lights of a city on a hill.

As Household Lamps

Christians are also like ancient lamps. Jesus says, "Neither do people light a lamp and put it under a bowl. Instead they put it on its stand, and it gives light to everyone in the house" (Matthew 5:15). The point is unmistakable, for the principal function of a household lamp, and of a believer, is to provide illumination. Here the simple metaphor tells us so much:

Light reveals things as they really are. All of us have at some time walked into an unfamiliar room and have felt our way to the lamp and turned on the light, discovering a room far different from what we imagined.

Light promotes life. We all know that our summer patio plants will flourish in the basement during winter if we provide them with enough light. Even our broken bones mend faster if we can soak up some sunlight. Light is life-giving.

Light is persistent. It constantly assaults the surface of the earth and will penetrate the slightest crack. The darkest place is not safe from it if the tiniest opening appears.

Light awakens. Have you ever heard the sun rise? In a sense you can! In a quiet place in the country the rising sun can be heard as it calls nature awake. This is the way it is with spiritual light.

As lamps, the Divine Householder places us strategically. "Neither do people light a lamp and put it under a bowl. Instead they put it on its stand." The light is placed so it can shine to its best advantage. We are simply to shine where we have been placed. In fact, in the darker and less promising places our light may have the greatest effect.

God has made us *visible* like a city on a hill, and He has made us to *illumine* life like a lamp in a dark room. He has placed us where He knows we can shine to His best advantage. Our presence is to reveal life, sin, and goodness as it is, and to provide a light that draws others to it like a summer lamp.

The Spiritual Responsibility Light Brings

The *fact* and *function* of light in our lives brings a vast *responsibility*. Our Lord is explicit about this: "Let your light shine before men, that they may see your good deeds and praise your Father in heaven" (Matthew 5:16). This is a command, not a suggestion. With urgency in His voice Christ says, "If you are light, then shine!" May we all keep the emotion of this imperative before us!

The medium of shining, He tells us, is our "good deeds." The word He uses for "good" is *kalos*, which bears the idea of attractiveness or beauty, rather than the more common *agathos*, which means "good in quality." Jesus wants our light to shine through beautiful, attractive works. Of course, He is not recommending self-conscious, staged works. Yet He does suggest that if our works are seen, then let them be beautiful. Our Lord would thus tell us that acts of compassion and caring are at the top of the list. John Stott explains:

> Indeed, the primary meaning of "works" must be practical, vis-
> ible deeds of compassion. It is when people see these, Jesus said,
> that they will glorify God, for they embody the good news of

His love which we proclaim. Without them our Gospel loses its credibility and our God His honor.[5]

And why should we be given to beautiful, shining works? Jesus' answer is radiantly clear: that they may "praise your Father in heaven." All glory to God! *Soli Deo Gloria.* As David said, "Not to us, O LORD, not to us but to your name be the glory, because of your love and faithfulness" (Psalm 115:1).

To Shine Like Christ

"You (you alone) are the light of the world"—this is thrilling! It suggests that we can become like Him in relation to this world. We would not have dared to say it, but He did—to our everlasting amazement.

As light, as part of Him, we are sure to prevail. Ultimately He will completely vanquish the forces of darkness.

> *As by the sun in splendor*
> *The flags of night are furled,*
> *So darkness will surrender*
> *To Christ who lights the world.*[6]

To Shine Forever

In eternity we will be part of the light ourselves. Jesus said at the end of the Mystery Parables, "The righteous will shine like the sun in the kingdom of their Father" (Matthew 13:43). That means us! C. S. Lewis once noted that the heavens only reflect the glory of God. But we share the glory of the Father with Christ. And we shall be more glorious than the heavens.

Nature is mortal. We shall outlive her. When all the suns and nebulae have passed away, each one of you will still be alive.

Nature is only the image, the symbol. . . . We are summoned to pass in through nature beyond her to the splendor which she fitfully reflects.[7]

As Christians there is a glory awaiting us that involves, in some mysterious way, shining. We do not know how that will be. Somehow we are going to enter into the light of the approval of God, and we will be glorious beings, far beyond all imagination.

To Shine Now

But right now Jesus says, "You are the light of the world."

Let us covenant with all our being to shine as brightly as possible in this dark world.
Let us covenant to expose ourselves to the face of Jesus in prayer.
Let us covenant to be visible for Him.
Let us covenant to shine where He has placed us.
Let us covenant to do beautiful works.

NOTES

Chapter 1: *Are Evangelicals Born Again?*

1. Walter A. Elwell, ed., *The Evangelical Dictionary of Theology*, R. V. Pierard, "Evangelicalism" (Grand Rapids, Mich.: Baker, 1984), p. 379. See also George Marsden, ed., *Evangelicalism and Modern America* (Grand Rapids, Mich.: Eerdmans, 1984), pp. vii-xix.
2. David Wells, *No Place for Truth or Whatever Happened to Evangelical Theology?* (Grand Rapids, Mich.: Eerdmans, 1993), p. 134.
3. *Christianity Today*, "The Christianity Today-Gallup Poll: An Overview," December 21, 1979, pp. 14-15.
4. Wells, *No Place for Truth*, pp. 135, 293.
5. Dietrich Bonhoeffer, *The Cost of Discipleship* (New York: Macmillan, 1969), p. 47.
6. Wells, *No Place for Truth*, pp. 54, 78, 87.
7. James Davison Hunter, *Evangelicalism: The Coming Generation* (Chicago: University of Chicago Press, 1987), p. 69.
8. Wells, *No Place for Truth*, pp. 163, 166.
9. Hunter, *Evangelicalism: The Coming Generation*, p. 73.
10. Robert Schuller, *Self-Esteem: The New Reformation* (New York: Jove, 1985), pp. 98, 99.
11. Doug Murren, *The Baby Boomerang* (Ventura, Calif.: Regal, 1990), pp. 102, 103.
12. Hunter, *Evangelicalism: The Coming Generation*, p. 63.
13. *Ibid.*
14. Doug Sherman and William Hendricks, *Keeping Your Ethical Edge Sharp* (Colorado Springs, Colo.: NavPress, 1990), pp. 29-31.
15. Os Guinness, *The Gravedigger Files* (Downers Grove, Ill.: InterVarsity Press, 1983), pp. 130-139.
16. Donald Bloesch, *Crumbling Foundations* (Grand Rapids, Mich.: Zondervan, 1984), p. 91, says: "The striking resurgence of evangelicalism in America may be an Indian summer before the total collapse of organized religion in this country."
17. Tryon Edwards, *The New Dictionary of Thoughts* (San Diego, Calif.: Classic Publishing House, 1931), p. 251.
18. D. A. Carson, *The Sermon on the Mount* (Grand Rapids, Mich.: Baker, 1978), p. 16.

Chapter 2: The Riches of Poverty

1. Charles Colson, *Who Speaks for God?* (Wheaton, Ill.: Crossway Books, 1985), p. 153.
2. John R. W. Stott, *The Message of the Sermon on the Mount* (Downers Grove, Ill.: InterVarsity Press, 1979), p. 33.
3. D. A. Carson, *The Sermon on the Mount* (Grand Rapids, Mich.: Baker, 1978), p. 16.
4. D. Martyn Lloyd-Jones, *Studies in the Sermon on the Mount*, Vol. 1 (Grand Rapids, Mich.: Eerdmans, 1959), p. 47.
5. Carson, *The Sermon on the Mount*, p. 17.
6. Edward H. Sugden, ed., *John Wesley's Fifty-three Sermons* (Nashville: Abingdon, 1983), pp. 231-232.
7. David F. Wells, *No Place for Truth or Whatever Happened to Evangelical Theology?* (Grand Rapids, Mich.: Eerdmans, 1993), p. 183.
8. R. Kent Hughes, *Romans: Righteousness from Heaven* (Wheaton, Ill.: Crossway Books, 1991), pp. 89-96, where the author expands Paul's logic that salvation is by *faith alone* in respect to Abraham ((vv. 1-5), David (vv. 6-8), the Gentiles (vv. 9-12), the Law (vv. 13-15)—*sola fide* (v. 16).
9. George L. Lawlor, *The Beatitudes Are for Today* (Grand Rapids, Mich.: Baker, 1974), pp. 40-41.

Chapter 3: The Comfort of Mourning

1. Charles Colson, *Who Speaks for God?* (Wheaton, Ill.: Crossway Books, 1985), pp. 136-137.
2. *Ibid.*, p. 137.
3. C. H. Spurgeon, *Lectures to My Students* (Grand Rapids, Mich.: Zondervan, 1969), p. 166.
4. Oswald Sanders, *Spiritual Leadership* (Chicago: Moody Press, 1967), p. 60.
5. Edward H. Sugden, ed., *John Wesley's Fifty-three Sermons* (Nashville: Abingdon, 1983), p. 239.
6. Thomas F. Roeser, "There Is One Thing Worse Than Sin," *Chicago Sun-Times*, August 22, 1983.
7. George L. Lawlor, *The Beatitudes Are for Today* (Grand Rapids, Mich.: Baker, 1974), pp. 40-41.
8. Colson, *Who Speaks for God?*, p. 138.

Chapter 4: The Strength of Gentleness

1. William Henley, "Invictus," in *The Home Book of Verse*, selected and arranged by Burton E. Stevenson, 9th edition (New York: Henry Holt & Co., n.d.), pp. 3500-3501.
2. Colin Brown, *The New International Dictionary of New Testament Theology*, Vol. 2 (Grand Rapids, Mich.: Zondervan, 1979), pp. 256-257.

3. William Barclay, *A New Testament Wordbook* (New York: Harper & Brothers, n.d.), p. 103.
4. M. R. Vincent, *Word Studies in the New Testament* (Gainesville, Fla.: Associated Publishers and Authors, 1972), p. 30.
5. Barclay, *A New Testament Wordbook*, p. 104.
6. Hugh Martin, *The Beatitudes* (New York: Harper & Brothers, 1953), pp. 44- 45.
7. D. Martyn Lloyd-Jones, *Studies in the Sermon on the Mount*, Vol. 1 (Grand Rapids, Mich.: Eerdmans, 1959), p. 69.

Chapter 6: **The Dividend of Mercy**

1. John R. Claypool, *The Preaching Event* (Waco, Tex.: Word, 1980), p. 39.
2. *Ibid.*, pp. 37-40.
3. Robert Guelich, *The Sermon on the Mount* (Waco, Tex.: Word, 1982), pp. 88-89.
4. Haddon Robinson, *Biblical Preaching* (Grand Rapids, Mich.: Baker, 1980), p. 150.
5. Corrie ten Boom, *The Hiding Place* (Grand Rapids, Mich.: Chosen Books, 1971), p. 215.

Chapter 7: **The Reward of Purity**

1. Reprinted in *Chicago Sun-Times*, February 17, 1982.
2. William Barclay, *A New Testament Wordbook* (New York: Harper, n.d.), p. 69.
3. D. Martyn Lloyd-Jones, *Studies in the Sermon on the Mount*, Vol. 2 (Grand Rapids, Mich.: Eerdmans, 1959), p. 111.

Chapter 8: **The Paternity of Peace**

1. Will and Ariel Durant, *The Lessons of History* (New York: Simon & Schuster, 1968), p. 81.
2. *Ibid.*, p. 86.

Chapter 9: **The Joy of Persecution**

1. William Blake, "The Auguries of Innocence" (lines 59-62), *The Complete Poetry and Prose of William Blake*, revised edition, ed. David V. Erdman (Berkeley, Calif.: University of California Press, 1982), p. 491.
2. Hugh Martin, *The Beatitudes* (New York: Harper & Brothers, 1953), p. 75.
3. Joseph Bayly, *The Gospel Blimp* (Richardson, Tex.: Windward Press, 1969), p. 32.
4. Dietrich Bonhoeffer, *The Cost of Discipleship* (New York: Macmillan,1969), pp. 100-101.

Chapter 10: **Coming to Christ**

1. Philip Yancey, *Where Is God When It Hurts?* (Grand Rapids, Mich.: Zondervan, 1977), p. 32.

2. William Barclay, *The Gospel of Matthew*, Vol. 2 (Philadelphia: Westminster, 1958), p. 301.
3. Richard Chenevix Trench, *Notes on the Miracles of Our Lord* (Grand Rapids, Mich.: Baker, 1956), p. 135.
4. Colin Brown, *The New International Dictionary of New Testament Theology*, Vol. 2 (Grand Rapids, Mich.: Zondervan, 1979), pp. 875-877.
5. Brooke Foss Westcott, *Christian Aspects of Life* (New York: Macmillan, 1897), p. 354.

Chapter 12: Be Salt!

1. W. Philip Keller, *Salt for Society* (Waco, Tex.: Word, 1981), p. 100.
2. William Barclay, *The Gospel of Matthew*, Vol. 2 (Philadelphia: Westminster, 1958), p. 116.
3. Malcolm Muggeridge, *Christ and the Media* (Grand Rapids, Mich.: Eerdmans, 1977), p. 46.
4. F. W. Boreham, *A Bunch of Everlastings* (New York: Abingdon, 1920), p. 186.

Chapter 13: Be Light!

1. *The Mishna*, Sukkah 5:2-3, trans. Herbert Danby (New York: Oxford, 1974), p. 180.
2. Shakespeare, *Macbeth*, Act 1, Scene 5, lines 55-58.
3. James M. Boice, *The Sermon on the Mount* (Grand Rapids, Mich.: Zondervan, 1972), p. 80.
4. D. Martyn Lloyd-Jones, *Studies in the Sermon on the Mount*, Vol. 1 (Grand Rapids, Mich.: Eerdmans, 1959), p. 174.
5. John R. W. Stott, *The Message of the Sermon on the Mount* (Downers Grove, Ill.: InterVarsity, 1979), p. 62.
6. James Hastings, ed., *Speaker's Bible*, Vol. 6 (Grand Rapids, Mich.: Baker, 1971), p. 108.
7. C. S. Lewis, *The Weight of Glory* (Grand Rapids, Mich.: Eerdmans, 1965), p. 13.

SCRIPTURE INDEX

Luke

1:46-47	26-27
2:8-15	27
2:14	87
2:25-38	27
4:18	26
5:12	109, 113
6:35	90
10:25-28	66
10:30-37	70
10:36-37	63
11:13	123-124
15:18-20	42
18:1-6	120
18:10-14	30, 69-70
22:29-30	59
23:34	46

John

2:14-17	47
3:6	79
3:7-8	79
3:19	138-139
4:10	60
4:14	59
6:35	59
8:12	138
14:13	49
14:27	88
15:3	80
15:18-20	99

Acts

5:41	96
14:22	99

Romans

1:17	54
3:9	121
3:10-12	36
3:13-14	36
3:15-17	36
3:21-22	54

5:1, 10	91
8:17	48
8:26-27	124
11:6	28, 80
12:18	86
14:19	86

1 Corinthians

6:2	48
6:9-11	91
6:20	23
7:23	23
7:35	74

2 Corinthians

3:18	78, 141
4:17	103
5:21	115
12:9-10	29

Galatians

5:19-21	91
5:23	49

Ephesians

2:6	29
2:7a	80
2:7	49
2:8-9	28, 65
2:13-17	88
4:3	86
5:8	140

Philippians

2:3-8	89
2:12-13	80
3:9	54
3:10	58

Colossians

1:19-20	88, 91
2:9-10	29

1 Thessalonians
3:3-4   99

1 Timothy
1:15   40

2 Timothy
1:12   58
3:12   99
4:7-8   103

Titus
2:11-14   81

James
2:13   65
3:17-18   87
4:2   118, 125

4:8   74, 80

1 Peter
1:19   88
2:23   46
2:24   116

2 Peter
1:4   140

1 John
3:2-3   80
3:17   66
5:14   49

Revelation
3:17-18   28
3:20   21

GENERAL INDEX

Accommodation, cultural, theological, moral, 12-14
Africa, 130
Ahab, 35
Ammon, 35
Amusing Ourselves to Death (Neil Postman), 38
Amusement, cultural overdose on, 38
Anna, 27
Applause of Heaven, The (Max Lucado), 23
Aristotle, 45
Asia Minor, 135
Augsburg Confession, 100
Auguries of Innocence (William Blake), 95
Augustine, 135

Barclay, William, 73
Barnhouse, Dr. Donald Grey, 139
Bayly, Joseph, 97
Beatitudes, the
  "attitudes of grace" (Hughes), 17
  function of, 17-19
  their sublime benefit, 76
Be Happy Attitudes, The (Robert Schuller), 13
Believers, counterfeit, 11, 16
Bernard of Clairvaux, 58
Blake, William, 95
Blessedness see *Jesus Christ, smile of*
Bonhoeffer, Dietrich, 11, 99
Born again, 9 (Chapter 1 *passim*), 79
Boswell, James, 133
Brand, Dr. Paul, 110

Carter, Howard, 117-118
"Cheap grace," definition of, 11
Chesterton, G. K., 34
Chicago Sun-Times, 39

Christianity, evangelical see *Evangelicalism*
Church, the
  as preservative, 130-132
  as spice, 132-133
  as thirst stimulator, 133
  resalting, 134-135
  when becomes tasteless, 133-134
Colson, Charles, 33, 34, 42
Crane, Congressman Daniel, 39

David Copperfield (Charles Dickens), 24
David, King, 26, 36, 56, 77, 144
Devotion to God, 73-76
Dickens, Charles, 24
Dinur, Yehiel, 33-34
Discipleship, 100
Divine feast, 59
Durant, Ariel, 83
Durant, Will, 83

Ecuador, 141
Egyptians, 138
Eichmann, Adolf, 33-34
Emancipation Bill, 133
England, 130, 133
Ephraimites, 14
Evangelical, the term, 10-11
Evangelical, the title, 14-15
Evangelicalism, 10, 12, 13, 15
Evangelicalism: The Coming Generation (James Davison Hunter), 12
Evangelicals, 11, 14, 57
Ezekiel, 73,85

Faith, 114, 116
"Felt needs," preaching to, 13